THE PRAYER OF OUR LORD

OTHER CROSSWAY BOOKS BY PHILIP GRAHAM RYKEN

Courage to Stand
Discovering God in Stories from the Bible
Is Jesus the Only Way?
Jeremiah and Lamentations
When You Pray

WITH JAMES MONTGOMERY BOICE

The Heart of the Cross
Jesus on Trial
The Doctrines of Grace

THE PRAYER OF OUR LORD

PHILIP GRAHAM RYKEN, D. PHIL.

CROSSWAY BOOKS

A PUBLISHING MINISTRY OF
GOOD NEWS PUBLISHERS
WHEATON, ILLINOIS

ACKNOWLEDGMENT

The publisher wishes to acknowledge that *The Prayer of Our Lord* is adapted and condensed from the previously published book by Philip Graham Ryken, *When You Pray*, published by Crossway Books in 2000.

The Prayer of Our Lord

Copyright © 2002 by Philip Graham Ryken

Abridged from *When You Pray: Making the Lord's Prayer Your Own*, copyright © 2000 by Philip Graham Ryken.

Trade paperback edition, 2007

Published by Crossway Books
        a publishing ministry of Good News Publishers
        1300 Crescent Street
        Wheaton, Illinois 60187

Cover design: Jessica Dennis

Cover photo: iStock

First printing, trade paper, 2007

Printed in the United States of America

ISBN 13: 978-1-58134-921-4

ISBN 10: 1-58134-921-1

Unless otherwise designated, Scripture is taken from *The Holy Bible: New International Version®*. Copyright © 1973, 1978, 1984 by International Bible Society. Used by permission of Zondervan Publishing House. All rights reserved.

The "NIV" and "New International Version" trademarks are registered in the United States Patent and Trademark Office by International Bible Society. Use of either trademark requires the permission of International Bible Society.

Scripture identified KJV is taken from the King James Version of the Bible.

Library of Congress Cataloging-in-Publication Data

Ryken, Philip Graham, 1966-
   The prayer of our Lord / Philip Graham Ryken.
      p.   cm.
   Includes bibliographical references.
   ISBN 1-58134-388-4 (HC : alk. paper)
   1. Lord's prayer—Criticism, interpretation, etc. 2. Spiritual life—Christianity. I. Title.
BV230 .R94   2002
226.9'606—dc21   2002001408

VP		17	16	15	14	13	12	11	10	09	08	07
15	14	13	12	11	10	9	8	7	6	5	4	3	2	1

To Kirsten Elisabeth Ryken,

*in the hope that she will learn to talk
with her heavenly Father
like Mor-Mor and Grandmary*

Contents

FOREWORD

This little book is about the greatest prayer in the Bible—the prayer that our Lord Jesus gave to his disciples.

But more than this, it is about the pattern for prayer that Jesus has given to you and to me, so that we may discover peace and contentment, hope and forgiveness, truth and assurance that comes from God alone through prayer.

How simple yet deeply profound the Lord's Prayer is, as we can see even in brief outline:

—The fatherhood of God (and his loving care for his children);
—The holiness of God (and his holy sacrifice for us);
—The kingdom of God (and his reign over all of life);
—The will of God (and his perfect plan for us);
—The provision of God (day by day for all our needs);
—The forgiveness of God (for all sins and the sins of others);
—The protection of God (from temptation and from Satan's power); and
—The reality of his kingdom, his power, and his glory forever.

This little book then, by God's grace, holds the promise of changing your life and my life—to help us live day by day and moment by moment in loving dependence on God. Think, for example, of the dramatic part the Lord's Prayer played in overcoming evil during the tragic events of September 11, 2001—how after Todd Beamer prayed the

Lord's Prayer, "God enabled Todd and his fellow passengers on Flight 93," as Todd's widow Lisa Beamer writes, "to take courageous actions that undoubtedly saved many lives."

May we indeed be challenged and encouraged always to pray, as Lisa writes further:

> On September 11, Todd's mission on earth was completed, and he ended daring greatly. . . . Our challenge in the time remaining for us is to each day dare greatly for God, leaving lukewarm faith behind.
>
> I covet your prayers now and in the future as my children and I face the challenges of life each day without Todd. I thank you in advance for the blessings these will bring for us.
>
> I pray, too, as you face the challenges of each day that you will know that you are never without hope, through faith that is founded in the sovereign, loving God.[1]

As you read the words of this book, may the greatest prayer of the Bible bring you deeper understnding of the living God, and of his power and his presence and his peace, so that you may "dare greatly for God, leaving lukewarm faith behind." *For thine is the kingdom, and the power, and the glory, forever. Amen.*

Lane T. Dennis, Ph.D.
President and Publisher
Crossway Books

1

How to Pray

This then is how you should pray: "Our Father which art in heaven, hallowed be thy name. Thy kingdom come. Thy will be done in earth, as it is in heaven. Give us this day our daily bread. And forgive us our debts, as we forgive our debtors. And lead us not into temptation, but deliver us from evil: For thine is the kingdom, and the power, and the glory, for ever. Amen" (Matthew 6:9-13 KJV).

Our Family Prayer

The Lord's Prayer is a family prayer for all God's children. There are three important ways in which this is true. The first is the most obvious: In the Lord's Prayer we pray to our Father. No one can learn to pray who does not learn to call God

"Father." That is what prayer is: It is talking with our heavenly Father. Our fundamental identity as Christians is as sons and daughters of the Most High God. Therefore, when we pray, we address God as Father.

There is a second sense in which the Lord's Prayer is a family prayer. The Father to whom we pray is called *our* Father. This means that when we pray, we are joined by our brothers and sisters. Because this is something we learn from the precise wording of the Lord's Prayer, it is important to realize that there is more to the Lord's Prayer than mere words. Jesus was teaching his disciples *how* to pray, not *what* to pray. He did not say, "Pray *this*:" and then give the exact words we always have to use in our prayers. Instead he said, in effect, "Pray like this," or "Pray in this manner."

The Lord's Prayer is a flexible pattern or framework for prayer. Hugh Latimer, an English reformer who was martyred for his faith, said, "this prayer [is] the sum and abridgment of all other prayers. All other prayers are contained in this prayer; yea, whatsoever mankind hath need of as to soul and body, that same is contained in this prayer."[1]

Even though Jesus gave his disciples a prayer to imitate rather than a prayer to memorize, he *did* give us specific words to use when we pray. Since he undoubtedly chose his words with care, it is important to notice what he repeats over and over again: the first-person plural pronouns "our" and "us." "*Our* Father." "Give *us*." "Forgive *us*." "Deliver *us*." The Lord's Prayer is for the whole family of God.

Someone has written a clever poem to help remind us that the Lord's Prayer is not for rugged individualists:

> *You cannot pray the Lord's Prayer*
> *And even once say "I."*
> *You cannot say the Lord's Prayer*
> *And even once say "My."*
> *Nor can you pray the Lord's Prayer*
> *And not pray for another,*
> *For when you ask for daily bread*
> *You must include your brother.*
> *For others are included*
> *in each and every plea—*
> *From the beginning to the end of it,*
> *It never once says "Me!"*[2]

God does not expect us to maintain the life of prayer in our own strength. Jesus knows how weak we are. Therefore, when he teaches us to pray, he invites us into fellowship. What he has given us is a family prayer, a prayer we must be taught by another Christian. Furthermore, the prayer itself assumes that we will have company when we pray. When we pray to our Father, we will be joined by our spiritual brothers and sisters.

PRAY WITH YOUR BROTHERS AND SISTERS

Jesus often took a small group of disciples with him when he went off to pray. To this day, Jesus calls his disciples to come away in small groups to pray, for wherever two or three come together in his name, he is right there with us (Matt. 18:20).

Since the Lord's Prayer is a family prayer, we not only pray *with* one another, but we also pray *for* one another. In the last three petitions we do not pray for ourselves primarily but for the whole church.

When we say, "Give us today our daily bread," we are praying for *our daily provision*. We are asking God to meet the material needs of our brothers and sisters. Jesus taught us to pray for the needs of the family.

We are also to pray for *our daily pardon*, which is what we do when we say, "Forgive us our debts." Some sins are private sins. They are committed by an individual within the privacy of the heart. While every Christian needs to confess his or her own personal sin, other sins are corporate sins. They are committed by nations, cities, churches, or families. They are no one's fault in particular, but they are everyone's fault in general. When we pray the Lord's Prayer, we confess not only our individual sins, but especially the corporate sins of the church. What are the prevailing sins of your church? Pride? Hypocrisy? Prejudice? Greed? These are the kinds of sins that require corporate repentance.

Finally, when we say, "Lead us not into temptation, but deliver us from evil," we pray for *our daily protection*. As a pastor, I offer this kind of prayer on behalf of my congregation: "Some of us will be tempted to sin today, Lord. Keep us from falling. Provide a way of escape. Save us from sin and from Satan!" Daily provision, daily pardon, daily protection—these are the things we ask for in our family prayer.

PRAY LIKE YOUR OLDER BROTHER

There is one final sense in which the Lord's Prayer is a family prayer. It is a prayer we learn from our Older Brother.

If we are the children of God, then Jesus Christ is our Older Brother. It only makes sense. Since Jesus is God the Son—the unique, eternally begotten Son of God (John 1:18; 3:16)—God the Father is his Father. But God the Father is also *our* Father by adoption. When we accept the death and resurrection of Jesus Christ for our sins, we become the children of God. Therefore, we share the same Father with Jesus, which makes us his younger brothers and sisters.

What does this have to do with the Lord's Prayer? It means that Jesus prays the Lord's Prayer with us and for us. When Jesus prayed "Our Father," he meant *our* Father, the God who is our Father as well as his. The God and Father of our Lord Jesus Christ is also our Father in heaven. The Lord's Prayer, therefore, is the family prayer that we learn from our Older Brother.

Consider how many of these petitions were first uttered by Jesus Christ. "*Our Father which art in heaven.*" This is how Jesus always prayed. Whenever we overhear him praying in the Gospels, he addresses God as Father: "I praise you, Father, Lord of heaven and earth" (Luke 10:21); "My Father, if it is possible, may this cup be taken from me" (Matt. 26:39). Sometimes he even says, "Holy Father" (John 17:11), which is another way of saying, "Hallowed be thy name."

"*Thy will be done, on earth as it is in heaven.*" This was the prayer of Jesus' whole life. "I have come down from heaven not to do my will," he said, "but to do the will of him who sent me" (John 6:38). Jesus came to do his Father's will on earth, as he had done it in heaven, even when it included suffering and dying for our sins on the cross. In the Garden of Gethsemane, on the eve of his crucifixion, Jesus was "overwhelmed with sorrow to the point of death" (Matt. 26:38). He even asked if the cup of suffering could be taken away. "Yet," he prayed, "not as I will, but as you will" (Matt. 26:39). In other words, "Thy will be done." And God's will *was* done! It was the will of heaven that the Son should die on the cross for sins. Therefore, when Jesus was crucified, God's will was done on earth as it had been decreed in heaven.

"*Give us this day our daily bread.*" This, too, was Jesus' prayer. He knew that man does not live on bread alone (Matt. 4:4), and yet he still needed to eat his daily bread. Thus we find Jesus praying at mealtimes. He looked up to heaven and prayed before he fed the five thousand (John 6:11). He did the same thing before he gave bread to his disciples at the Last Supper (Matt. 26:26). Jesus did not provide daily bread without first praying for it.

But what about "*Forgive us our debts*"? It is true that Jesus did not have any debts of his own. Yet the reason Christ came into the world was to assume all of our debts upon the cross: "The LORD laid on him the iniquity of us all" (Isa. 53:6b); "God made him who had no sin to be sin for us" (2 Cor. 5:21). When Jesus died on the cross, was he not asking his Father— at least with his actions, if not with his words—to forgive us our debts? Furthermore, even while he was asking God to forgive our debts, Jesus forgave his debtors. While they were hurling insults at him, he said, "Father, forgive them, for they do not know what they are doing" (Luke 23:34).

Jesus also taught his disciples to say, "*And lead us not into temptation, but deliver us from the evil one.*" Jesus prayed that we would be delivered from Satan, saying to his Father, "protect them from the evil one" (John 17:15). Jesus prayed this way for Simon Peter, knowing that he would fall under spiritual attack and deny him three times. Jesus said, "Simon, Simon, Satan has asked to sift you as wheat. But I have prayed for you, Simon, that your faith may not fail" (Luke 22:31-32a).

Finally, Jesus prayed for God's kingdom, power, and glory. The kingdom of God is what Jesus came to bring. It is what he preached and what he promised, perhaps even what he prayed for. He certainly prayed for God's power and glory: "Father, the time has come. Glorify your Son, that your Son may glorify you. . . . Holy Father, protect them by the power of your name" (John 17:1, 11b).

In one way or another, Jesus prayed nearly every petition in the Lord's Prayer. He taught his disciples to pray this way because it was the way *he* prayed. Think of the Lord's Prayer as a "pre-owned prayer." It comes to us second-hand, tried and tested by our Older Brother. And when Jesus made these petitions, his prayers were answered. God's name was hallowed, his kingdom has come, and his will is being done. Through the death and resurrection of Jesus Christ, God the Father forgives our debts and delivers us from the Evil One.

If God has answered the prayers of our Lord, he will answer us when we pray the Lord's Prayer. If you are a child of God, use your family prayer. Pray with your brothers and sisters, the way your Older Brother always did. Your Father is ready to listen.

2

OUR FATHER IN HEAVEN

The one who taught us the most about the fatherhood of God was God's own Son, who instructed us to pray using these words: "Our Father in heaven" (Matt. 6:9). With these words, Jesus introduced a completely new way to pray. Kent Hughes writes:

> God is only referred to as "Father" fourteen times in the huge corpus of the Old Testament's thirty-nine books—and then rather impersonally. In those fourteen occurrences of "Father," the term was always used with reference to the nation, and not individuals. God was spoken of as Israel's Father, but Abraham

did not speak of God as "my Father." You can search from Genesis to Malachi, and you will not find such an occurrence.[1]

Jesus was the first person to make the fatherhood of God so essential to prayer. He calls God "Father" some sixty times in the Gospels. Calling God "Father" was the heart of the prayer life of Jesus Christ as it was for no one before him.

ABBA, FATHER

Jesus was also the first to employ the precise word that he used when he addressed his Father. It was the word Jewish children used for their fathers: *abba*. In fact, *abba* was almost certainly the word that Jesus himself used for his father Joseph when he was working in his carpentry shop back in Nazareth.

The word *abba* was picked up by the apostles and used by the first Christians when they prayed. This was a completely new development in the history of prayer. There is no record of anyone else ever having addressed God in such a familiar way. It may have seemed rather presumptuous. Who did Jesus think he was, calling God his Father? Of course Jesus knew exactly who he was . . . the eternal Son of God. Therefore, he prayed, "*Abba*, Father," addressing God in a way that no one else would dare.

The way Jesus prayed was remarkable. What is more remarkable is that he made it possible for us to pray the same way. First, he made us God's sons and daughters: "To all who received him [Jesus], to those who believed in his name, he [God] gave the right to become children of God" (John 1:12). By trusting in Jesus Christ to save us from sin and death, we are born again as children of God. We are adopted into God's family.

Once we become children of God, the Holy Spirit enables us to call God Father: "Because you are sons, God sent the Spirit of his Son into our hearts, the Spirit who calls out, '*Abba*, Father'" (Gal. 4:6).

PRAY WITH CONFIDENCE

How does a child speak to his father? Children who love their fathers approach them with both the warmest confidence and the deepest reverence. Both of these attitudes are expressed in the Lord's Prayer—confidence and reverence for God the Father.

First, when we pray to God as our Father, we draw near to him with confidence. This confidence comes from intimacy, from knowing that our Father is also our friend.

Sadly, fathers are not always known for intimacy. We are now living in what David Blankenhorn calls *Fatherless America*.[2] Some fathers are absent; they have abandoned their families. Other fathers are weak; they fail to provide spiritual leadership in the home. Still others are distant; they do not show affection to their families. So we have forgotten, perhaps, who a father is and what he does. But a real father is a man who has a passionate love for his family. Because of the warmth of his affection—not only for his children, but especially for their mother—his children have the confidence to ask him for what they need.

Some people find it difficult to approach God with confidence because they have never known a father's love. In the providence of God, they never had a father who blessed them. He was absent, he was detached and disapproving, or he was angry and violent. As a result, nearly the last thing they want to do is to give their heart to someone they have to call "Father."

Yet Jesus teaches us to call God "our Father," and to do so with confidence, even if we have never known a father's love. This is because Jesus knows that a father's love is what we have always longed for. He invites us to become God's beloved children. He teaches us to speak to him as our dear Father. That may be difficult at first, but as we learn to pray to God as our Father, we experience the healing that only the Father's love can bring.

PRAY WITH REVERENCE

Jesus teaches us to pray "*Abba*, Father" so that we will come to God with the confidence of a child. But we do not approach God without reverence. He is our Father in heaven. He dwells in a high and lofty place of majesty, power, and dominion, where he is worshiped by myriads upon myriads of angels.

This fact ought to make a great difference when we pray. Christians sometimes forget that the fatherhood of God demands their reverence. It is often said that the best translation of the Aramaic word *abba* is something like "daddy." After all, "daddy" is the word small children use for their fathers in English. If *abba* is the word small children used for their fathers in Aramaic, then "daddy" it is.

However, *abba* does not mean "daddy." The Oxford linguist James Barr has proven that *abba* was not merely a word used by small children.[3] It was also the word that Jewish children used for their parents after they were fully grown. *Abba* was a mature, yet affectionate way for adults to speak to their fathers.[4]

The New Testament is careful not to be too casual in the way it addresses God. The Aramaic word *abba* appears three times in the English New Testament (Mark 14:36; Rom. 8:15; Gal. 4:6). In each case, it is followed immediately by the Greek word *pater*. *Pater* is not the Greek word for "daddy." The Greek language has a word for "daddy"—the word *pappas*—but that is not the word the New Testament uses to translate *abba*. Instead, in order to make sure that our intimacy with God does not become an excuse for immaturity, it says, "*abba, pater*."

The best way to translate *abba* is "Dear Father," or even "Dearest Father." That phrase captures both the warm confidence and the deep reverence that we have for our Father in heaven. It expresses our intimacy with God, while still preserving his dignity. When we pray, therefore, we are to say, "Our dear Father in heaven."

WHAT ARE FATHERS FOR?

We come to God with both reverence and confidence. But what do we come *for*? We come for what children usually come to their fathers for. In the last petitions of the Lord's Prayer, we ask for exactly the kinds of things that children ask from their fathers: provision, pardon, and protection.

First, we pray for *provision*. We beg God, "Give us today our daily bread." Providing daily bread is part of a father's job. He is the breadwinner. He is a "good provider," people say. God the Father is not only a good provider; he is the best provider of all.

Second, we ask our Father for *pardon*. We pray, "Forgive us our debts, as we also have forgiven our debtors" (Matt. 6:12). Granting pardon is also part of a father's job. When children are really naughty, they usually have to answer to their fathers.

Jesus once told a story about a son who returned to his father to ask for pardon (Luke 15:11-32). The key to the whole story is the first word out of the son's mouth: "Father." "The son said to him, 'Father, I have sinned against heaven and against you'" (Luke 15:21). What gave the son the confidence to go home and seek pardon for his sins was that he was going home to his father.

In much the same way, it is the fatherhood of God that

gives us the confidence to ask God to pardon our sins. Like the wayward son, we say, "Father, I have sinned against you." This is part of the logic of the Lord's Prayer. We would never have the courage to ask God to forgive us our debts (in the fifth petition) unless we already knew that we could call him our Father (from the opening address). The reason we pray to God as our Father—and the reason our Father will forgive us—is because Jesus has paid for our sins through his death on the cross.

Finally, we pray for *protection*. We ask our Father to "lead us not into temptation, but deliver us from the evil one" (Matt. 6:13). In making this petition, we are asking God to defend us from sin and from Satan. Defending the family is another part of a father's responsibility. He is a protector as well as a provider.

Everything we really need—provision, pardon, protection—depends on the fatherhood of God. God is our loving Father, and so he is willing to help us. He is our Father in heaven, with infinite resources at his disposal. So he is also able to help us. Now Jesus invites us to draw near to him, confidently and reverently, asking him for what we need and calling him, "Dearest Father."

3

HOLY IS
YOUR NAME

The Lord's Prayer compels us to acknowledge God's bright and burning holiness. From the very beginning, it directs our thoughts toward God and his perfections. First comes the address, in which we cry to our Father in heaven. Yet lest we approach him too casually, the first petition reminds us that he is a *holy* Father: "Hallowed be your name." As we begin the asking part of our prayer, then, the first thing we beg God to do is to make his name holy.

WHAT'S IN A NAME?

To be holy is to be set apart in purity. It is to be separated from what is common and ordinary in order to be devoted to

God's service. Whatever is holy is distinguished from the secular and dedicated to the sacred.

When we say that God is holy, we do not simply mean that he does not sin. He does not, of course. God's holiness does have an ethical dimension. The Bible says that "the holy God will show himself holy by his righteousness" (Isa. 5:16b). God is undefiled in all his ways. He is the supreme, the superlative moral majesty in the universe. But God's holiness refers to more than his ethics. Holiness refers to everything that distinguishes the Creator from his creation. It is the infinite distance between his deity and our humanity. Holiness is the very Godness of God, the sum total of all his glorious perfections.

God is so holy that everything associated with him is holy, including his name. These days most people think that names are relatively unimportant. "What's in a name?" Romeo asked Juliet.

Romeo was wrong, however, because it takes the right name to convey the essence of the thing. This is why the Old Testament people of God took names so seriously. They did not name their children after sports figures, soap opera stars, or Disney characters. They gave them names that would reflect the essence of their divine calling. They understood that a name is not a label; it is an identity. People do not just *have* names; they *are* their names.

This is especially true when it comes to the holy name of God. God's name expresses his person; it reflects who he is.

The name is God himself, as he has made himself known to us. It reveals his divine nature and his eternal qualities. God is who his name is, and his name deserves the highest praise. Jeremiah said, "No one is like you, O LORD; you are great, and your name is mighty in power" (Jer. 10:6). David sang, "O LORD, our LORD, how majestic is your name in all the earth!" (Ps. 8:1a). He was echoing the seraphim, who always sing, "Holy, holy, holy is the LORD Almighty; the whole earth is full of his glory" (Isa. 6:3).

SANCTIFY YOUR NAME

We are starting to understand what Jesus meant when he taught us to pray, "Hallowed be your name." What does it mean to be holy? To be holy is to be set apart in purity. What is God's name? It is the sum total of his character. But what does it mean for God's name to be hallowed?

What we are asking God to do in this petition is to satisfy his own chief end, which is to glorify himself. God is hallowed whenever he shows that he is holy. When we ask him to hallow his name, therefore, all we are doing is asking him to reveal that he is exactly who he is. Since God is holy, and his name is holy, to ask God to make his name holy is simply to ask him to live up to his name. "Hallowed be your name" means "Make yourself known as the Holy One that you are." It is a prayer for God to display the Godness of his Godhood.

In particular, in the first petition of the Lord's Prayer, we are asking God's name to be hallowed by ourselves and by other human beings. The petition thus has an evangelistic purpose. God's name is hallowed when human beings declare that he is holy. So we are praying that his creatures will come to give him the honor that he deserves. What better way to begin our prayers? When we get on our knees, the first thing we ask of God is to glorify himself, to show that he is utterly transcendent in his holiness. We pray that God would be given that unique reverence that his nature and character demand.

A HOLY SACRIFICE

In order for us to come into God's holy presence, something has to be done about our sin. King David asked, "Who may ascend the hill of the LORD? Who may stand in his holy place?" (Ps. 24:3). His answer was, "He who has clean hands and a pure heart" (Ps. 24:4a). But this is exactly our problem. We have filthy hands and impure hearts. We are as *un*holy as God is holy. Therefore, we find ourselves keeping our distance, standing at the bottom of the hill, not daring to ascend and meet with God in his holy place.

We cannot hallow God until God hallows us, which he does through his Son Jesus Christ, the Holy One of God. Jesus came to this earth to give his life as a holy sacrifice for sin. As the time of his crucifixion drew near, he said, "Now my heart is troubled, and what shall I say? 'Father, save me from this hour'? No, it was for this very reason I came to this hour. Father, glorify your name!" (John 12:27-28a). Jesus died on the cross to glorify his Father's name. In other words, the way

Jesus hallowed God's name was by suffering and dying for our sins.

Once it was God's holiness that separated us from God, the holiness of his being. Now it is God's holiness that brings us to God, the holiness of the perfect sacrifice Jesus offered for our sins on the cross. God displayed his holiness by making us holy through his holy Son.

A HOLY LIFE

If Christ died to make us holy, then holy we must be. Consider the surprising word the New Testament uses over and over to describe God's people. The word is *saint*, which means "holy one." It is significant that the Greek noun for *saint* comes from the same root as the Greek verb "to hallow." This means that one of the places God hallows himself is in us! He answers the first petition of the Lord's Prayer by "sanctifying" his "saints," or "hallowing" his "holy ones."

Note how baptism bears witness to the holiness of God's name. After all, Christians are baptized in the *name* of the Father, the Son, and the Holy Spirit (Matt. 28:19). Not only are we baptized into this name, but we are also sanctified by his name: "You were washed, you were sanctified, you were justified in the name of the Lord Jesus Christ and by the Spirit of our God" (1 Cor. 6:11). Now that God has placed his name on us, he is known to be holy whenever we are holy. The Scripture thus gives us this command: "Let him who is holy continue to be holy" (Rev. 22:11). If we bear the name "Christian," we must become what we are: set apart for God in purity. We *are* holy because of what Jesus Christ has done *for* us. But we must continue to *be* holy by what his Spirit does *in* us.

We ask God to make us holy in our actions. We must not use the parts of our bodies to do what is immoral or shameful. Instead, we use our feet to spread the Gospel, our hands to feed the poor, and our arms to lift up the weak.

We ask God to make us holy in our words. We must not curse or use coarse language. The reason this kind of talk is called "profanity" is because it profanes God's name (see Lev. 22:31-32). Instead of cursing, we use our mouths for blessing. And when we speak about spiritual things, we do it reverently, not with words that sound pious, but with genuine piety.

We ask God to make us holy in our thoughts. We must not fill our minds with things that are violent or indulge in sexual fantasy. Instead, we use our minds to contemplate the holiness of God and the purity of everything he has made.

We ask God to make us holy in our emotions. To put it negatively, we must put away our unrighteous anger and our self-pity. To put it positively, we must put on the emotions of Jesus Christ. We are to love the things he loves and hate the things he hates, to be brokenhearted for the things that break his heart.

We ask God to make us holy in our worship. When we worship God properly, we leave off seeking a name for ourselves and begin to seek the honor of his name. We make known to ourselves and to others that God's name is holy.

To summarize, we are to pray that God would make us holy in everything we do, say, think, feel, and adore. "Just as he who called you is holy, so be holy in all you do; for it is written: 'Be holy, because I am holy'" (1 Pet. 1:15). This is the whole task of the Christian life: to become what God is in his holiness. In other words, to hallow his name.

Happily, this is a prayer that God intends to answer. His plan is to reveal more and more of his perfection until the whole earth is full of his holiness: "From the west, men will fear the name of the LORD, and from the rising of the sun, they will revere his glory" (Isa. 59:19).

The Puritan Thomas Watson had a beautiful thought about this prayer. His thought was that "Hallowed be your name" is the one petition that God's people will continue to make for all eternity:

> When some of the other petitions shall be useless and out of date, as we shall not need to pray in heaven, "Give us our daily bread," because there shall be no hunger: nor, "Forgive us our trespasses," because there shall be no sin; nor, "Lead us not into temptation," because the old serpent is not there to tempt: yet the hallowing of God's name will be of great use and request in heaven; we shall be ever singing hallelujahs, which is nothing else but the hallowing of God's name.[1]

We will join with the voices of angels, who never stop saying, "Holy, holy, holy is the Lord God Almighty, who was, and is, and is to come" (Rev. 4:8b).

4

YOUR KINGDOM COME

Sometimes it is hard to believe that God's kingdom will ever come. The world is troubled by poverty, injustice, and war. The Gospel seems to make little progress from one day to the next. The wicked triumph while the righteous go about in chains. When we see all this, we do not stop praying for the kingdom, but we do want to ask God, "When will your kingdom come?"

KINGDOMS IN CONFLICT

To understand the slow coming of God's kingdom, it helps to remember that almost from the very beginning, there have really been two kingdoms. Augustine wrote about them in his great work *The City of God.* He said there are two king-doms: the kingdom of God and the kingdom of man. Each of these two kingdoms has its own ruler, its own people, its own desire, and its own destiny.

The kingdom of God is ruled by Almighty God, and its people are all his loyal subjects. Their heart's desire is for God himself and for his glory. The ultimate destiny of that kingdom is to rule on earth as it does in heaven. Yet over against God's kingdom stands the kingdom of this world, ruled by Satan. Its subjects are men and women born in rebellion against God. They love only themselves, to the contempt of their Creator. Thus their evil kingdom is destined to fail. One day it will be swallowed up in the victory of God. But in the meantime, Satan and his followers battle God's kingdom at every turn.

THE COMING OF THE KING

In one sense, God has always been the King: "The LORD has established his throne in heaven, and his kingdom rules over all" (Ps. 103:19); "His dominion is an eternal dominion; his kingdom endures from generation to generation" (Dan. 4:34b). This universe has never been a democracy; it has always been an absolute monarchy, for God has always been on the throne.

Yet God's kingship has also been a matter of endless dispute. God has always had to fight to defend his sovereign rule against the kingdom of darkness. Even now an invisible battle rages between God and Satan for the souls of men and women. We see the casualties all around: abuse, addiction, hatred, injustice, and war. No wonder it takes so long for the kingdom to come! There are two kingdoms, not one, and God's kingdom cannot come without Satan's kingdom being destroyed.

It takes a king to establish a kingdom, which is why God sent Jesus into the world: "The reason the Son of God appeared was to destroy the devil's work" (1 John 3:8b). And destroy it he did. He not only preached the kingdom, but he practiced it: "Jesus went through Galilee teaching in their synagogues, preaching the good news of the kingdom, and healing every disease and sickness among the people" (Matt. 4:23; cf. 9:35). By performing these kingdom miracles, Jesus was overthrowing Satan's kingdom. Every time he cast out a demon, healed a disease, or raised the dead, he was undoing the work of the devil. "If I drive out demons by the Spirit of God," Jesus said on one occasion, "then the kingdom of God has come upon you" (Matt. 12:28). In this way God's King began to restore God's rule over God's creation.

THE KING REJECTED

The more Jesus established God's kingdom, the more people started to treat him like a king. The crescendo of their praise built to a great climax when he rode into Jerusalem. The people gave him a royal welcome, spreading their garments in his path and shouting, "Blessed is the coming kingdom of our father David!" (Mark 11:10a); "Blessed is the king who comes in the name of the Lord!" (Luke 19:38a).

Before they could proceed to the coronation, however, Satan still had one or two tricks to play. There was still the chance that he could persuade people to reject God's kingdom. Satan did this by persuading them to wish for the wrong kind of king. Although the people of Jerusalem were longing for God's kingdom to come, they did not understand what kind of kingdom it was.

In the first place, people misunderstood God's *plan* for his kingdom, although the fact that Jesus was riding on a donkey should have given them a clue. They thought the kingdom would come the way kingdoms usually do—by military force. But Jesus had a different strategy. The kingdom of God would not come by power and might, but through suffering and death.

Second, people misunderstood the kingdom's *purpose*. They conceived of God's kingdom in political terms. They wanted Jesus to drive out the Romans. But God had a different purpose. He wanted to conquer the real enemies of humanity—sin, death, and the devil—and to establish his rule in the hearts of his people.

Third, people misunderstood the *progress* of the kingdom. They thought God's kingdom would come right away, which meant that their timing was off. They were right to wave their palms and shout "Hosanna!" The kingdom *was* coming. However, it would take more than a few days to get there. Sadly, most of them were not willing to wait. Before the week was out, they were calling for Jesus to be executed. Humanly speaking, it was people wishing for the wrong kind of kingdom that got Christ crucified.

PRAYING FOR GOD'S KINGDOM

How can we come to a better understanding of God's kingdom? One of the best ways is by learning how to pray, "Your kingdom come." These three simple words from the Lord's Prayer explain the plan, the purpose, and the progress of God's kingdom.

In the first place, this petition helps us to understand God's *plan* for ushering in his kingdom. The very fact that we are to pray for the kingdom proves that it is not the kind of thing we establish through our own efforts. It is something we must ask God to do because only he can do it.

God's plan was to establish his kingdom through his Son. His kingdom comes mainly through proclamation, through the announcement that Christ, who was crucified, is now King. The reason the church tries so many other things besides preaching Christ is because it suspects the kingdom can be established in some other way. But there is no other way. People will not come into the kingdom because they like the minister, support the children's program, or enjoy the music. They may come into a church that way, but not into the kingdom. The only way people ever come into God's kingdom is by hearing his heralds proclaim a crucified King.

When we hear the glad news that Christ is King, the thing to do is submit to his rule. When we repent for our sins and believe in Jesus Christ, God establishes his rule in our hearts. This is part of what Jesus meant when he said "the kingdom of God is within you" (Luke 17:21). Anyone who has ever entered that kingdom has done so by praying, "Your kingdom come," or words to that effect. That is the way the kingdom comes to us and the way we come into the kingdom. To become a Christian is simply to ask God to set up his throne as the supreme King of our hearts. It is to say, as Frances Havergal said, "Take my heart, it is thine own; it shall be thy royal throne."

SEEKING GOD'S KINGDOM

The second petition of the Lord's Prayer also says something about the kingdom's *purpose*. We pray, "*Your* kingdom come," and thus we ask for *God's* kingdom to come, not our own.

A king has the right to rule his kingdom any way he likes, and God's kingdom is a kingdom of the heart. It is not a territory. It is not a party politic. It is not a nation-state with geographic borders. The kingdom of God is simply the rule of God. When we pray for God's kingdom to come, we are asking God to achieve his purpose of reigning as King in the hearts, minds, and wills of his loyal subjects.

Once we understand God's purpose for his kingdom, we can see that he wants to bring all of life under his sovereign rule. It is through the common activities of daily life that God establishes his uncommon kingdom. Whenever we calculate the accounts payable, double-check a lab result, haul away the trash, serve a hot meal to the homeless, finish our homework, help a customer find the right size, water the geraniums, or snap the lid on a sippy-cup, we are doing kingdom work. We are doing kingdom work provided, that is, that we do whatever we do in submission to God's rule, for the sake of his royal honor. We are doing kingdom work, not because doing these things will change the world, necessarily, but because by doing them we show how God has changed us.

Seeking the kingdom also means praying for God to establish his rule around the world. It means asking God to use pastors, evangelists, missionaries, and church planters, and even ourselves to spread the Gospel that transforms sinful rebels into loyal subjects. Anyone who comes under God's gracious rule wants to see everyone else come under it as well, until the kingdom of Christ covers the earth as the waters cover the sea.

KINGDOM COME

The last thing the Lord's Prayer helps us understand is the *progress* of God's kingdom. The petition "Your kingdom come" reminds us that the kingdom is not here yet, at least not in all its fullness. Otherwise, why would we still pray for it to come?

In one sense, of course, the kingdom has already come because Jesus has come, and he is the King. But his rule has yet to spread to its widest extent. The kingdom of God, one might say, is "a once and future kingdom." We are not praying for it to come into existence, but to come to dominance.

The progress of God's kingdom is gradual. It does not come all at once. We should not be discouraged, therefore, when we look at the world around us and see how, in so many ways, the kingdom of God is not yet here. The troubles of the world simply send us back to our knees where we offer the prayer Jesus taught us to pray. We are still praying for the kingdom of Christ to overcome the kingdom of this world.

The coming of the kingdom has often been compared to the way the Allies defeated Germany in the 1940s. For all intents and purposes, World War II was over on D-Day when British and American troops established a beachhead in France. There were still great battles to be fought, of course, and lives would be lost. But from that point on, the Nazis were fighting a losing battle. All that remained was for the Allies to liberate Europe.

As far as the kingdom of God is concerned, D-Day was Good Friday. That was Satan's last mad attempt to have God's King betrayed, tried, and nailed to the cross. But Satan was only able to wound him. By dying on the cross for our sins, Jesus was actually striking a death blow to sin, death, and the devil. Now the outcome of the battle between the two kingdoms is certain. All that remains is for God to liberate the captives of Satan's kingdom and bring them into the kingdom of his Son.

We should not be surprised if the kingdom seems to come slowly. But it will come. Make no mistake about that! Jesus even promised that it would come soon (Rev. 22:12). And as we wait for its coming, the prayer we often find on our lips is the last prayer in the whole Bible: "Come, Lord Jesus" (Rev. 22:20). This is another way of praying the second petition of the Lord's Prayer: "Thy kingdom come."

One day that prayer will be fully answered. Jesus Christ will come again as King to establish the "dominion that will not pass away and the kingdom that will never be destroyed" (Dan. 7:14). He will gather all his loyal subjects around his throne, and he will say to them, "Come, you who are blessed by my Father; take your inheritance, the kingdom prepared for you since the creation of the world" (Matt. 25:34). Then the King will destroy the dominion of the devil and all his unholy followers. The trumpets of angels will sound, and loud voices from heaven will say, "The kingdom of the world has become the kingdom of our Lord and of his Christ, and he will reign for ever and ever" (Rev. 11:15). Hallelujah! Amen.

5

YOUR WILL BE DONE

Imagine a work force comprised entirely of angels. Not fallen angels who hate God and his work, but perfect angels who always serve him with joyful praise. Angels on the payroll— it would be every employer's dream, for there are no slackers in heaven! Angels are God's best servants because they always do what he says. Whatever the command, they say, "Thy will be done," and then they do it. By obeying God's every word, they make sure that his divine will is done in heaven.

BACK DOWN TO EARTH

When we pray the way Jesus taught us to pray, we ask God to help us do his work on earth the way the angels do it in heaven: "Your will be done, on earth as it is in heaven" (Matt. 6:10). This is the third petition in the Lord's Prayer. It is the last of the "thy" petitions: "Hallowed be *thy* name, *thy* kingdom come, *thy* will be done." Up to this point, the prayer has been all about God. We have prayed for God's name, God's kingdom, and God's will. But from this point on we will pray for ourselves—our provision, our pardon, and our protection. It is the third petition that brings the Lord's Prayer down to earth, making the transition from our Father up in heaven to his children down on earth.

In one sense, of course, God's will is always done. How could it be otherwise? Since God is all-powerful, he does whatever he purposes to do. It is the very Godness of God to do whatever he pleases.

By his will God created the universe: "For you created all things, and by your will they were created" (Rev. 4:11). Having made this world, God does with it whatever he wills. The psalmist wrote, "The LORD does whatever pleases him, in the heavens and on the earth, in the seas and all their depths" (Ps. 135:6).

God also does what he wills in redemption. From beginning to end, the whole plan of salvation unfolds according to the will of his eternal decree: "In love he predestined us to be adopted as his sons through Jesus Christ, in accordance with his pleasure and will" (Eph. 1:5). Having willed to save his people, it is God's will to keep us safe to the very end. Jesus said, "And this is the will of him who sent me, that I shall lose none of all that he has given me, but raise them up at the last day" (John 6:39).

And when that day comes, the will of God will be done on earth as it is now done in heaven. His will *must* be done! For the Bible teaches that God is the one "who works out everything in conformity with the purpose of his will" (Eph. 1:11). Therefore, our prayer for God's will to be done cannot go unanswered.

*M*Y *W*ILL *B*E *D*ONE?

In the meantime, God's revealed will is not always done. Otherwise, why would we need to pray for it? We live in a world where people do not obey the revealed will of God's command.

We ourselves are part of the problem. In our sinful nature, we do not want to obey the command of God's revealed will. In fact, we want the very opposite. We do not seek after God, do not love him, and will not obey him. Whether we are with our family or our friends, whether we are at work or at rest, we want to have our own way rather than God's way.

Consider the mistake my friend made during a worship service. As he was singing the Lord's Prayer, he became aware that people had turned around to look at him in astonishment. Suddenly he realized what had happened. He had just sung, as loudly and as joyfully as he could, "*My* kingdom come, *my* will be done!" Whether we realize it or not, this is often the way we come to God in prayer. Deep down, what we really want is for God to let us have our own way.

We need the third petition of the Lord's Prayer to show us how wrong it is to think of prayer as a way of getting something from God. Imagine what a mess our lives would be in if God always did what we wanted him to do! For unlike God's will, our own wills are evil, displeasing, and imperfect. It is much better for us to yield to the sovereign purpose of our loving heavenly Father, who really does know best!

THE ONE WHO CAME TO DO GOD'S WILL

Be forewarned that it is not always safe to pray the Lord's Prayer. When we pray, "Your will be done," we are yielding to God his right to do as he pleases. Often that means praying for things we are not sure we want or may not want at all. "Thy will be done" is the kind of prayer that might lead to suffering and even to death.

Consider what happened to the only man who ever totally surrendered to God's will: Jesus Christ. Jesus always did what God told him to do. His only purpose in life was to submit to the will of his Father in heaven. "My food," said Jesus, "is to do the will of him who sent me and to finish his work" (John 4:34). For Jesus, doing God's will was life itself.

Throughout his life Jesus always fulfilled the will of his Father. But his last and greatest surrender was to death. The Bible teaches that Jesus "became obedient to death—even death on a cross" (Phil. 2:8). To understand the cost of that obedience, one has to go to the Garden of Gethsemane where Jesus prayed the night before he was crucified.

The prayers Jesus offered that night were sheer agony. In the garden Jesus wrestled with God's will for his life and his death. "My Father," he prayed, "if it is possible, may this cup be taken from me" (Matt. 26:39). Jesus knew what kind of cup it was, the cup of God's wrath against sin. So if ever a man wrestled with God's will, it was Jesus Christ, the God-man. Yet out of the depths of his woe, Jesus prayed the very prayer he has taught us to pray: "My Father, if it is not possible for this cup to be taken away unless I drink it, may your will be done" (Matt. 26:42).

After he had said his prayers, Jesus allowed himself to be handed over to unjust men. They had him betrayed, tried, convicted, mocked, beaten, and executed. Yet through these terrible events Jesus' prayers were answered. God's will *was* done. For it was the Father's will that the Son should suffer and die for our sins. The crucifixion was not a tragic mistake; it was God's plan for the salvation of sinners. It was God's plan that Jesus should be nailed to the cross and thus to die for our sins. And because it was God's plan, it was the answer to the prayer Jesus made for God's will to be done.

HAVE THINE OWN WAY, LORD

The way God answered Jesus' prayers in the Garden of Gethsemane was unique. It had to do with the once-and-for-all salvation of the world. But Jesus has given us permission to use his prayer, and just as his submission is the model for our surrender, so his petition is the pattern for our prayers.

In what specific ways is God calling us to pray for his will to be done? First, we must submit to God's will for our salvation. To pray, "Your will be done," is to admit that we need to be saved. For when we pray for God to do his will, we are admitting that we do not always do it. And if it is true that we do *not* do God's will, then we are sinners, and therefore in need of salvation. Submitting our will to God's will begins with putting our faith in Christ. It means believing that Jesus died on the cross for our sins and trusting that he was raised from the dead to give us eternal life.

Submitting to God's will for our salvation is only the beginning, however. When we pray, "Your will be done," we are committing ourselves to God's will for every aspect of life and death. We are adopting God's agenda and throwing away our own.

In what other ways should we pray for God's will to be done? Submitting to God's will means accepting the way God made us, with all our strengths and weaknesses, and thus embracing who we are in Christ. In his book *The Spiritual Life of Children*, Harvard sociologist Robert Coles describes meeting a little girl from Mississippi. The child had just drawn her self-portrait in crayon. She pointed to it and explained, "That's me, and the Lord made me. When I grow up my momma says I may not like how He made me, but I must always remember that He did it, and it's His idea."[1]

If you were the Creator, you might have made "you" differently. But God has made us for his own pleasure. Every aspect of our personality, every feature of our appearance, every part of our body, every one of our talents and limitations has been given according to his exact specifications. The proper way to respond to the way God has made us is to say, "Lord, if this is who you made me to be, then your will be done."

Submitting to God's will means going wherever he sends us, to do whatever he calls us to do. If we are his servants, then he has a job for us to do in his kingdom. But if we want to know what God wants us to do, the first question is not, "What is God's will for my life?" as if we have to read God's mind to know what we ought to do. Really, the first question about God's will is, "Am I willing to do it?" There is no sense asking God to reveal his will unless we are committed to doing what he wants done. This is where the Lord's Prayer helps us. Even though we do not know God's will for our future, we can still pray about it. And the more we pray for God's will to be done, the more we yield ourselves to it.

THROUGH SUFFERING, INTO GLORY

Submitting to God's will means accepting whatever suffering God brings into our lives. This, too, is part of his will. As it was for Christ, so it is for the Christian: God will not save us *from* suffering, but *through* suffering into glory.

One woman who surrendered to God's will was Betty Stam, a missionary to China. Betty and her husband, John, were captured by Communists, stripped half-naked, and marched in chains through the streets of their village. Betty was forced to watch as her captors chopped her husband's head off. Then she herself was beheaded. Many years before her horrific martyrdom, Betty Stam wrote the following prayer: "Lord, I give up all my own plans and purposes, all my own desires and hopes, and accept thy will for my life. I give myself, my life, my all utterly to thee, to be thine forever. Fill me and seal me with thy Holy Spirit. Use me as thou wilt. Send me where thou wilt, and work out thy whole will in my life at any cost, now and forever."[2] As Betty Stam's prayer illustrates, when we pray for God's will to be done, we are praying for his will to be done in *everything*. We are submitting to his will in all the circumstances of both life and death.

In the meantime, we long for the day when we will be with God in his glory, when we will be unwilling to sin, when with all the saints and angels we will finally do God's will as it is done in heaven. While we still live on earth and not in heaven, we pray for God to do with us what he wills and to make of us what he chooses, in order to glorify himself as he pleases.

What pleases God is nothing less than our total surrender. Are you ready to submit to God? John Wesley wrote a wonderful prayer of surrender to God's will. If you want God's will to be done in your life, then make it your prayer as well: "I am no longer my own, but yours. Put me to what you will, rank me with whom you will; put me to doing, put me to suffering; let me be employed for you or laid aside for you, exalted for you or brought low for you; let me be full, let me be empty; let me have all things, let me having nothing; I freely and wholeheartedly yield all things to your pleasure and disposal."[3]

6

GIVE US TODAY
OUR DAILY BREAD

Once we have prayed for God's heavenly glory, then it is right for us to pray for our own earthly good: "Give us this day our daily bread." This simple petition is profound in its teaching about God and its implications for the Christian life. Each word has something important to teach us.

GIVE . . .

First, there is the word *give*, which shows that even the most basic necessities of life are a gift from God. Most of us have such an abundance of bread that we forget to pray for it. Some years ago a publisher wrote an essay to explain why he had given up on prayer. "I don't pray anymore," he admitted. "I've given it up for Lent. Also for Advent and Pentecost. . . . How can I maintain, without lying, that God has a hand in this meal?"[1]

The man's problem was that he couldn't see how God was the ultimate source of his provision. Yet the truth is that everything we eat is a divine gift. Praying for God to give us our daily bread, then, is a matter of fundamental honesty. God is the one who waters the earth and makes the crops to grow. He is the one who gives us life and strength to earn our bread and then to bake it. Thus our daily bread is not to be taken for granted. We are utterly dependent upon God's gracious provision every moment of every day.

. . . US . . .

The second important word is the easiest to miss: "Give *us* this day our daily bread." In the Lord's Prayer we are praying for God to meet the needs of our brothers and sisters.

It makes sense to pray for *our* bread because it takes a community to produce a loaf of bread. One person plows the field, plants the seed, and harvests the grain. Another person grinds the flour, and another bakes the bread. Still others deliver the loaf to the dinner table. Thus most of the bread we eat, at least in America, was made by someone else.

By asking God to give "us" our bread, we also identify with the poor, especially the Christian poor. In this culture of consumption we often forget the hungry. But we live in a needy world. There are places in Asia, Africa, the Middle East, and South America where our own brothers and sisters are starving. Food for the world is a matter for prayer.

When we pray for God to give us bread, we are also committing ourselves to share it when we get it. Otherwise our prayer is insincere. How can we pray, "Give us this day our daily bread," and then refuse to provide what the rest of "us" need? If we are to pray this prayer honestly, we must be willing to become part of its answer. Getting daily bread for oneself may seem like a physical matter, but giving daily bread to others is a spiritual matter. Therefore, we must feed the hungry. We must show hospitality to the homeless. We must send some of our bread to our brothers and sisters who have nothing to eat.

. . . TODAY . . .

The bread we ask God to give us all is bread for today. Here we come to the most difficult word in the entire prayer. The word is the Greek term *epiousion*, and the Lord's Prayer is the only place it appears in the entire New Testament (Matt. 6:11; Luke 11:3). Scholars have debated its meaning for centuries. The best translation is probably the one William Tyndale gave in 1525, and which English Bibles have used ever since: "daily bread." This translation was confirmed in 1925 when archaeologists discovered an ancient Egyptian papyrus with the word *epiousion*. The manuscript was an account of daily rations, almost like a grocery list. More recently scholars have found a papyrus from someone who ran errands to Alexandria to get some provisions, including *epiousion* and "other things pertaining to everyday life."[2] In both cases the word means "daily bread," just as it does in the Bible.

One of the things we discover as we read the Bible is that God's people often have to live one day at a time. After God led his people out of Egypt, he gave them bread from heaven, the manna in the wilderness (Exod. 16). The amazing thing about manna was that it could only be eaten that day. If it was kept overnight, it would spoil. This miracle showed that there are times when God's people have to live from hand to mouth, which is also the way the first Christians lived in Jerusalem. They were so poor that the apostles organized a daily distribution of food (Acts 6:1). By living from day to day, they learned to trust God constantly for everything.

Have you learned the same lesson? Do you live in daily dependence on God's provision? This does not mean that Christians always have to live at the subsistence level or may not plan for the future. What this petition does mean, however, is that we should not worry about the future. As Jesus later commanded, "Do not worry about tomorrow, for tomorrow will worry about itself" (Matt. 6:34). In his grace, God often gives us much more than we need, but sometimes his care for us will be "day-of." As far as our lives on this earth are concerned, all he has promised is daily bread.

. . . OUR DAILY BREAD

This brings us to the final word in this petition: *bread*. Actually, in the Greek original, the word *bread* comes first, for bread is what the petition is all about. A literal translation might go like this: "Our bread for the coming day, give us today."

What we are to pray for is bread, which is food reduced to its most basic level. Whether it comes in the form of a roll, a loaf, a cake, a bagel, a crumpet, a rice cake, or a tortilla, every culture in the world makes some kind of bread. It is one of the staples of life. When we ask God for bread, therefore, we are not asking for an extravagance.

The Bible uses the term *bread* to describe whatever food we really and truly need to live. Jesus teaches us to ask for bread, not dessert. Gregory of Nyssa explained it like this: "We are commanded to seek what is necessary for the preservation of the bodily existence, by saying to God, *Give bread*, not luxury, nor wealth, nor beautiful purple robes, nor ornaments of gold,—nor anything else by which the soul might be drawn away from its divine and worthier care, but—*bread*."[3]

Our trouble is that so often we come to God with our greeds rather than our needs. Already having everything we need, we pray for what we want. This then becomes the source of our discontent: We desire things that God has not promised. But in the fourth petition of the Lord's Prayer, Jesus teaches us that bread is enough for us. As the Scripture says, "If we have food and clothing, we will be content with that" (1 Tim. 6:8). Even if all we have is a little food to make it through the day, we still have all we need. And because bread is something we really do need, God will certainly give it to us.

It is the Father's pleasure to take care of the needs of his children. Remember that we are praying to our Father in heaven, who loves us in Jesus Christ. The petition for daily bread thus implies a promise, the promise that our Father will provide whatever his children actually need.

The great missionary to China, Hudson Taylor, learned about God's fatherly care from his own experience as a father. He wrote in one of his journals:

> I am taking my children with me, and I notice that it is not difficult for me to remember that the little ones need breakfast in the morning, dinner at midday, and something before they go to bed at night. Indeed I *could* not forget it. And I find it *impossible* to suppose that our heavenly Father is less tender or mindful than I. . . . I do not believe that our heavenly Father will ever forget His children. I am a very poor father, but it is not my habit to forget my children. God is a very, very good Father. It is not His habit to forget His children.[4]

The promise of God's fatherly provision is not just for bread; it is for all our everyday needs. "Bread" includes everything that is necessary for the body. It certainly includes clothing and perhaps shelter. It covers health and gainful employment and the strength and work we need to earn our daily bread. Whatever we truly need, God invites us to bring our requests to him.

THE BREAD OF LIFE

The bread we eat every day is a gift from God, a sign of his loving care for all his children. Yet for the Christian, bread can never be merely bread. Bread is a matter of life and death. We must eat to live. Therefore, the gift of our daily bread teaches us to depend on God for life itself, not only physically, but also spiritually.

Jesus tried to teach people this lesson after he fed the five thousand. They were so impressed with this miracle that they wanted to sign up for his permanent meal plan. "Sir," they said, "from now on give us this bread" (John 6:34). Jesus answered, "I *am* the bread." He was saying something like this: "You have to understand, there is more to life than daily bread. What you really need is life itself, not just now but forever, and I am the only one who can give it to you."

However real daily bread seems to us, it is not the reality; it is only the picture. Jesus Christ is the reality. Jesus said to them, "I tell you the truth, unless you eat the flesh of the Son of Man and drink his blood, you have no life in you. Whoever eats my flesh and drinks my blood has eternal life, and I will raise him up at the last day. For my flesh is real food and my blood is real drink" (John 6:53-55).

Jesus was speaking spiritually, of course. He was saying that what he did on the cross—offering his own body and blood for our sins—is the food and drink of eternal life. Anyone who wants to live forever with God must take Jesus in the way a hungry man takes in his daily bread. What joy there is to life when we discover that he is all we need, and that having him, we lack nothing! Jesus declared, "I am the bread of life. He who comes to me will never go hungry" (John 6:35).

7

FORGIVE US OUR DEBTS

The best thing to do when we fall into debt is to see a financial counselor. The first thing the counselor will do is calculate the full extent of our indebtedness. We have to know how much we owe before we can begin paying it. Since we find ourselves in God's debt, we need to know exactly how much we owe him.

IN GOD'S DEBT

There is a sense in which we owe everything to God. We owe him our existence. Our very lives are on loan from him, for he is the one who made us and sustains us. We are indebted to God for our gifts and talents, for our daily bread, and for every other good thing. Since we are God's creatures, we also owe him our perfect obedience.

The trouble with us, however, is that we do not glorify God and will not obey him. Therefore, we owe God a great debt because of our sin. We are guilty both for what we have done and for what we have left undone, for sins of commission as well as omission. Our debt includes secret sins as well as public ones, deliberate sins as well as sins committed in ignorance. We have not kept what Jesus called the two greatest commandments: love for God and love for our neighbor (Matt. 22:37-39). We have not loved God with all our heart, soul, mind, and strength. Nor have we loved our neighbors as ourselves, if we have loved them at all.

The two greatest commandments, in turn, can be divided into the Ten Commandments—four for the love of God and six for the love of neighbor. These we have broken as well. We have put other deities in God's place. We have cursed our Creator and the world he has made. We have been angry with people, even hated them. We have indulged in various kinds of sexual sin. We have taken things that did not belong to us, and we have stretched the truth. In short, we have sinned in every way, shape, and form, and every single sin adds to the sum total of our indebtedness.

When all our sins are added together, they place us in God's eternal debt. For we are obligated to keep God's law, and whenever we break that law, we become liable to its penalty—the wrath and curse of God. When we pray the way Jesus taught us to pray, therefore, we come as guilty sinners. We accept our legal status as God's debtors. We agree that we deserve to receive his just punishment for our sins.

MORE THAN WE CAN PAY

After figuring out exactly how enormous the debt is, the next thing is to set up a plan to begin paying it off. It is imperative to start making payments as soon as possible.

However, when we start trying to figure out how to pay God what we owe for our sins, we quickly realize how much trouble we are really in. Obviously, we cannot pay off our debt by ourselves. How could we ever make up for all the sins we have committed? Yet this is precisely the error most religions make, including every false version of Christianity. They all operate on the basis of something human beings can do to make things right with God.

The truth is, however, that forgiveness is not something we can work for; it is only something we can ask for. Even if we worked for all eternity, laboring in the very pit of hell, we could never work off the debt we owe to God. What could we ever pay to God? No one else can pay for us either, because everyone else has his own debts to worry about. The whole world is full of God's debtors. Asking someone else to settle our account with God would be like asking for a handout from a man heading for bankruptcy court!

DEAR DAD . . .

This is our financial condition, spiritually speaking: We owe God far more than we or anyone else could ever pay. So where can we turn for help?

Often when people get into real financial difficulty, they ask their parents for help. The Lord's Prayer works the same way. From beginning to end, the whole prayer is addressed to our Father in heaven. When we ask for our debts to be forgiven, therefore, we are asking our *Father* to forgive them.

Jesus once told a story about a young man who fell into debt. He was sick of home, tired of living under the authority of his father, and he decided to ask for his share of the inheritance before the old man died. Then he took the money and ran away from home. When he got to a far country, he squandered his wealth on wild living. Soon the young man's entire inheritance was spent, and he fell into bankruptcy.

In desperation the prodigal went out and did what his father probably had always wanted him to do: He started looking for a job. He was able to find a temporary position working on a hog farm. It was a miserable business, but he had no choice. Then one day, as he was slopping the pigs, his thoughts suddenly turned to his father's house. Jesus told the story like this: "When he came to his senses, he said, 'How many of my father's hired men have food to spare, and here I am starving to death! I will set out and go back to my father and say to him: Father, I have sinned against heaven and against you. I am no longer worthy to be called your son; make me like one of your hired men'" (Luke 15:17-19).

So the young man set off for home, hoping his dad would give him a job in the family business. There was only one flaw in his thinking: He underestimated his father's capacity for forgiveness. He was still thinking like a debtor, expecting to have to work off his debts. Then to the son's amazement, "While he was still a long way off, his father saw him and was filled with compassion for him; he ran to his son, threw his arms around him and kissed him" (Luke 15:20b).

Then the son made his little speech: "Father, I have sinned against heaven and against you. I am no longer worthy to be called your son" (Luke 15:21). But there was no talk then of becoming a hired hand. It was all robes and sandals, golden rings and fatted calves. There was no need for the son to slave away in his father's fields; he had been welcomed into the embrace of his father's forgiveness. For this is what forgiveness means: "To let go without a sense of guilt, obligation, or punishment."[1]

This is precisely what we ask God to do in the fifth petition of the Lord's Prayer. We ask our Father to forgive our debts. We declare our moral bankruptcy, freely admitting that we owe God more than everything we have. Then we do the only thing we can do, which is ask him to forgive us outright. Because he is our loving Father, God does what we ask. When we go to him, weighed down with the debt of all our guilt and sin, he does not sit down with us to work out a payment plan. Instead, he offers forgiveness full and free.

NAILED TO THE CROSS

When God remits our debts, he is well within his legal rights. The Scripture says that "if we confess our sins, he is faithful *and just* and will forgive us our sins" (1 John 1:9, emphasis mine). The reason God can justly forgive is because his children's debts have already been paid.

This is why Jesus Christ came into the world. God the Father grants us forgiveness through God the Son. He forgave our debt by personally nailing it to the cross: "He took it away, nailing it to the cross" (Col. 2:14). What makes this such a vivid image is that it corresponds to the way debts were sometimes cancelled in the ancient world. When a debtor finally paid off all his debts, his creditor would strike a nail through the certificate of debt. In the same way, when Christ died on the cross, God was driving a nail right through the infinite debt of our sin. Now there are no longer any outstanding charges against us.

Horatio Spafford had this image from Colossians in mind

when he wrote the triumphant third verse of the hymn "It Is
Well with My Soul":

> *My sin—O the bliss of this glorious thought!—*
> *My sin, not in part, but the whole,*
> *Is nailed to the cross, and I bear it no more;*
> *Praise the Lord, praise the Lord, O my soul!*

The debts we ask God to forgive when we pray the way
Jesus taught us to pray are the very debts that were crucified
with Christ at Calvary. When Christ died on the cross, all our
debts were cancelled. The Greek word for "cancel"
(*exaleipho*), which Paul used in Colossians 2, means "to blot
out" or "to wipe away." It means that the mountain of debt
we once owed to God because of our sin has been completely
removed.

RENEWING OUR REPENTANCE

This leaves us with an important practical question: Why do
we still need to ask for God's forgiveness? If all our debts have
been paid, why do we still need to be pardoned?

The Lord's Prayer makes asking forgiveness part of our
daily prayers. The fifth petition is joined to the fourth petition by the conjunction "and": "Give us today our daily bread,
and forgive us our debts" (Matt. 6:11-12). We need God to
"forgive us" as well as to "give us" every day. We are asking
him for daily pardon as well as daily provision. But how can
this be? God has already forgiven all our sins once and for all

through the death of Jesus Christ. Why then do we need to keep on asking for his forgiveness?

The answer, of course, is that we are not perfect and never will be on earth. We keep on sinning. We break God's commandments every day in thought, word, and deed. And although all our sins have been forgiven—past, present, and future—sin still has a way of disturbing our fellowship with God. It interferes with our intimacy with him, estranging us from his holiness. When we sin, therefore, our personal relationship with God needs to be restored. The Puritans called this "renewing our repentance." It means asking God to take the forgiveness he has already granted through Christ's death on the cross and to apply it freshly and directly to our sins.

To understand why we still need to ask for God's forgiveness in this way, it helps to remember that when we confess our sins, we are speaking to our Father. Once we are in Christ, our status as his children is never in jeopardy. But just because he is our Father, we need and want to ask for his forgiveness whenever we sin.

Once, when my son was a small boy, I tried to explain to him why we need the fifth petition of the Lord's Prayer. I said, "If you did something really, really naughty, would I ever throw you out of the house?" The idea sounded so preposterous to my son that he laughed. He knew that his place in his father's heart was absolutely secure. Then I said, "But you would still need to ask for my forgiveness, wouldn't you?"

He admitted that he would, because he had learned to prize his fellowship with his father. Jesus prizes our fellowship with his Father all the more. Although we are guilty sinners, he wants us to have the same kind of intimacy with the Father that he has. Thus he taught us to pray in these words: "Our Father in heaven . . . forgive us our debts."

8

As We Forgive Our Debtors

"To err is human, but to forgive is divine." This common expression reminds us that God has the capacity to forgive in ways that we do not—indeed, that we find it much easier to commit a sin than to forgive one.

Forgiven and Forgiving

We live in a cruel world where people do unspeakable things to one another. We are reminded of this every time we use the Lord's Prayer and say, "Forgive us our debts, as we forgive our debtors" (Matt. 6:12). From this petition we learn that we are not the only ones in debt. We have debtors of our own, people who owe us something for what they have done to us. And we are to forgive them.

What is hard to understand is the precise connection between our forgiveness and God's forgiveness. Jesus sensed that this petition would be the most difficult for his disciples to understand and apply. So he followed the Lord's Prayer with these words: "For if you forgive men when they sin against you, your heavenly Father will also forgive you. But if you do not forgive men their sins, your Father will not forgive your sins" (Matt. 6:14-15). It was almost as if to say, "Yes, you heard me correctly: 'Forgive us our debts, *as we also* have forgiven our debtors.'" This is a hard teaching. Yet it is the teaching of Jesus Christ.

The prayer for forgiveness is the only petition in the Lord's Prayer that comes with a condition attached to it. But we have so much trouble forgiving others that this condition immediately seems to throw our salvation into jeopardy. If we do not forgive, we will not be forgiven. Yet sometimes we find it seemingly impossible to forgive. How, then, can we be forgiven?

A famous statement from John Wesley illustrates our difficulty. As a young man Wesley was a missionary to Georgia, where he had a difficult time with the colony's founder, the proud and pitiless General Oglethorpe. During the course of one conversation, the general made this startling comment: "I never forgive." "Then I hope, sir," remarked Wesley, "you never sin."[1] Wesley was thinking of the fifth petition of the Lord's Prayer, which says there is no forgiveness for those who never forgive. The unforgiving are unforgiven.

GOD'S FORGIVENESS AND OUR FORGIVENESS

This petition does not mean that our forgiveness is equal to God's. The word *as* joins the two halves of the petition together and draws a comparison between God's forgiveness and our forgiveness. There is only a similarity, however, and not an identity, because God's forgiveness is much greater. The debts he forgives are infinite, whereas the ones we forgive are relatively small, even if they do not always seem that way to us. There also seems to be something significant about the fact that God forgives our *debts*, while we forgive our *debtors*. The most that we can do is pardon the sinner, not the sin. Only God can clear the actual charges of sin because he alone is the Judge of the universe.

Also notice which part of the petition comes first. Asking for our own forgiveness takes priority over offering it to others. If we had to forgive before we could be forgiven, then forgiveness would become a work, something we had to do to be saved. Yet we know that salvation comes by grace alone. Forgiveness is the free gift of God's mercy to all who believe. We cannot work off our debts; we can only ask for them to be canceled.

Those who are truly forgiven, truly forgive. The ability to

forgive is one of the surest signs of having been forgiven. If we have an unforgiving spirit, therefore, it shows that we have not taken to heart what it means to ask for and to receive God's forgiveness. The great English poet George Herbert explained why this must be so: "He that cannot forgive others, breaks the bridge over which he himself must pass if he would ever reach heaven; for every one has need to be forgiven."[2]

FORGIVE YOUR DEBTORS

If we must forgive, then how shall we do it? What does it mean to forgive our debtors?

It means to forgive everyone for everything. Forgive the neighbor who backed over your begonias. Forgive the sibling who colored in your books and the parent who never showed you very much affection. Forgive the spouse who doesn't meet your needs and the child who ran away from home. Forgive the coworker who stabbed you in the back and the boss who denied your promotion. Forgive the church member who betrayed a confidence or the pastor who gave you poor spiritual care. Forgive people for whatever they have done to you.

If you are a Christian, you do not have the right to withhold forgiveness from anyone for anything. The Bible says, "Forgive each other, just as in Christ God forgave you" (Eph. 4:32). To forgive, therefore, is to imitate God. It is to follow the example of Jesus, who even forgave his enemies while he was dying on the cross. In Christ there is grace to forgive the greatest sinners, from the uncle who molested you to the drunk driver who killed your son.

Forgiving our debtors means forgiving them even if they do not ask for our forgiveness. Debtors do not always know how indebted they are. Sometimes they know, but they don't care, and all we end up receiving is a half-hearted apology or maybe no apology at all. This is why there is such a big difference between forgiveness and reconciliation. It takes two to reconcile, so it is not always possible to be reconciled. But it takes only one to forgive. So if people do us wrong, we should forgive them, whether or not they ask for forgiveness. We cannot cancel their sin. Only God can do that, and he will only do it if they repent. But what we can do is set aside our own anger, bitterness, and resentment towards them. In other words, we can forgive them.

Forgiving our debtors means forgetting as well as forgiving. Sometimes it proves impossible to forget completely, of course. There are also times when it is necessary to hold people accountable for their actions. But forgetting means not holding on to a grudge. Forgiveness has to do with the attitude of the heart, and forgiveness that refuses to forget is no forgiveness at all. It is like the man who said he buried the hatchet, but he left the handle sticking out of the ground. That is not really forgiveness. True forgiveness means giving up my right to hurt you for what you have done to me.

Forgiving our debtors also means learning how to say, "I forgive you." Not "That's okay" or "Don't worry about it," but "I forgive you." When people ask for our forgiveness, it means that they have committed a sin. Forgiveness is the only response that calls sin a sin. Sin should not be overlooked, covered up, or ignored. It should be faced right up to and forgiven.

Forgiveness is often a process, particularly when the wounds are deep. What seems like full forgiveness at one time may later prove to have been incomplete. The thing to do in that case is to forgive all over again, and to continue to forgive as often as necessary. Like the rest of the Lord's Prayer, this petition is for everyday use. Since people sin on a daily basis, forgiveness is a part of daily life.

THE JOY OF FORGIVENESS

Offering radical forgiveness is not easy. It is not easy to forgive everyone for everything, to forget as well as to forgive, and to keep on forgiving over and over again. Forgiveness is very costly, and the more someone has hurt us, the harder it is to forgive. Here it helps to remember that we ourselves are debtors, and that therefore our forgiveness flows from God's forgiveness. If we have been forgiven, we can and we must forgive others as well as we can. We can forgive because God— who has forgiven all our debts in Jesus Christ—gives us the grace to forgive. We *must* forgive because it is vital to our own spiritual health.

Forgiveness brings great joy, not only to the forgiven, but especially to the forgiver. The Greek term for "forgiveness" (*aphiemi*) comes from a word that means "to let go." Forgiveness is a release, a letting go of self-destructive feelings such as anger, bitterness, and revenge. Those attitudes poison our intimacy with God and our harmony with other human beings. The only antidote for them is forgiveness.

The Christian writer and missionary Richard Wurmbrand once met a man who had experienced the divine release that comes through forgiveness. Wurmbrand was in a Communist prison in Romania at the time, lying in a cell reserved for those who were dying. In the cot on his right was a pastor who had been beaten so badly that he was about to die. On his left was the very man who had beaten him, a Communist who was later betrayed and tortured by his comrades.

One night the Communist awakened in the middle of a nightmare and cried out, "Please, pastor, say a prayer for me. I have committed such crimes, I cannot die." The pastor feebly sat up and called for another prisoner to help. Slowly he stumbled past Wurmbrand's cot and sat at the bedside of his enemy.

Wurmbrand watched as the pastor begin to caress the hair of the man who had tortured him. Then he spoke these amazing words: "I have forgiven you with all of my heart, and I love you. If I who am only a sinner can love and forgive you, more so can Jesus who is the Son of God and who is love incarnate. Return to Him. He longs for you much more than you long for Him. He wishes to forgive you much more than you wish to be forgiven. You just repent." There in the prison cell the Communist began to confess all his murders and tortures. When he had finished, the two men prayed together, embraced, and then returned to their beds, where each died that very night.[3]

The pastor had learned how to forgive from Jesus, who first forgave the pastor his own debts and then taught him to forgive his debtors.

9

LEAD US NOT INTO TEMPTATION

He heard it in the middle of the night. Long before the sun's first ray pierced the eastern horizon, he heard the sound that shattered his soul. It was only a shriek from the barnyard, the cry of an old rooster, but to his ears it must have sounded like the devil himself, crowing in triumph. For when Peter heard that noisy old bird, he "remembered the word Jesus had spoken: 'Before the rooster crows, you will disown me three times'" (Matt. 26:75).

Jesus was right. Thrice Peter denied his master. A night that began with the feasting of the Last Supper ended in profanity—desperate lies salted with the curses of an old sailor. Immediately, the rooster crowed, and Peter went out to weep bitter tears.

Jesus knew it would come to this, but there is a sense in which it was unnecessary. Peter did not have to deny his master. He would have had the courage to resist temptation if only he had remembered to pray the way Jesus taught him to pray: "Lead us not into temptation" (Matt. 6:13a). In case Peter had forgotten, Jesus reminded him of this petition that very night. In the Garden of Gethsemane he said to Peter, "Pray that you will not fall into temptation" (Luke 22:40). Unfortunately, Peter did not utter that prayer. He went to sleep instead. So when the temptation came, he fell right into it.

A Real Temptation

Peter's downfall shows that the sixth petition of the Lord's Prayer is crucial for the Christian life. We always stand in danger of sinning against our Savior, the way Peter did. We are in danger for two reasons. First, our enemy is strong—deadly strong, for our adversary is Satan himself. This is clear from the second half of the petition: "Lead us not into temptation, *but deliver us from the evil one*" (Matt. 6:13, emphasis added).

Consider what a powerful enemy Satan is. Peter himself later described him as a "roaring lion" who "prowls around . . . looking for someone to devour" (1 Pet. 5:8). The devil is relentless. No sooner have we resisted one temptation than his demons come after us with another. He is persistent. If we show the slightest sign of weakening, he will keep pressing us until we sin. He is crafty, gradually leading us down the road of destruction. He starts with a small temptation. When that succeeds, he presents us with a slightly greater temptation, slowly drawing us deeper and deeper into sin. He is subtle, so subtle that sometimes we find ourselves sinning before we are even aware of being tempted.

The devil is also deceptive. He lies about the true nature of sin. "You really need this," he says. "Just this once." "You can't help yourself." "It's not going to hurt anybody; so who cares?" "You know you're going to give in eventually; so go ahead and do it now, just to get it over with." "It will make you feel good!" With these and a thousand other falsehoods, the tempter goes about his deadly business. When Satan tempts you next, how will he do it? What strategy will he adopt? We are in mortal danger because our enemy is strong. He is the Evil One who wants to discredit our testimony, divide our family, and destroy our ministry.

The second reason we are in mortal spiritual danger is because we are so weak. We are sinners; therefore, sin is a real temptation for us. We are as prone to fall into sin as Peter was, if not more so. Our weakness explains why so many of our experiences with temptation involve failure. For most of us, it is easier to think of times we have fallen to temptation than to think of times we have stood firm. We are like Mr. Doolittle in the musical *My Fair Lady*. Mr. Doolittle is the immoral old man who explains, "The Lord above gave liquor for temptation, to see if man would turn away from sin. But," he sings, "with a little bit o' luck, with a little bit o' luck, when temptation comes, you'll give right in!"

That little song describes our spiritual condition apart from Christ. When temptation comes, we give right in. No Christian can withstand temptation in his or her own strength—not the teacher giving the Sunday school lesson, not the dear old woman praying for all the missionaries, and certainly not the minister standing in the pulpit. Nor can any group of Christians withstand temptation in their own strength—not the congregation wearing its Sunday best, not the school founded on solid biblical principles, and not even the family worshiping around the dinner table. Temptation is too dangerous for us to handle on our own.

PRAYING AGAINST TEMPTATION

If we are so weak, and our enemy is so strong, is there anything that we can do to withstand temptation? There are many ways to try and resist. One is to let someone else know that we are facing temptation. We can ask a brother or sister to pray for us, counsel us, and hold us accountable not to give in to a particular sin. Another way to resist temptation is to avoid all known occasions of sin. And when we do face temptation, we can defeat it by quoting Scripture just as Jesus did when he was tempted by Satan in the wilderness.

Those are all good ways to fight against temptation. But there is something else that must come first. Before getting a brother or sister to help, before avoiding the occasions of sin, and before fighting back with Scripture, we must pray the way Jesus taught us to pray. The very first thing to do in our struggle against sin, long before we even face temptation, is to pray for God to deliver us. That is why we need the last petition of the Lord's Prayer. We need to pray for our spiritual protection. If we could resist temptation in our own strength, this prayer would be unnecessary. But we cannot always resist. Thus we must ask God to do what we cannot do for ourselves, and that is to keep us from temptation.

What does it mean to ask God not to lead us into temptation? What exactly are we praying for?

The Greek word for "lead" means to "bring forcefully." It is like when a teacher grabs a student by the ear and "leads" him to the principal's office. So at first glance, it almost seems as if God is to blame for our temptations. But obviously that cannot be right. The Bible clearly teaches that God does not tempt anyone: "When tempted, no one should say, 'God is tempting me.' For God cannot be tempted by evil, nor does he tempt anyone" (James 1:13-14a). Yet the fact that God does not tempt us does not mean that our temptations are somehow outside his control. God is sovereign over all the affairs of life, including every temptation to sin. Although God does not tempt us, he does allow us to be tempted.

But what is meant by "temptation"? The Greek word for "temptation" can mean "test," "trial," "temptation," or even "tribulation." Although the sixth petition may include tests and trials of various kinds, it primarily refers to temptation to sin. When we pray, therefore, we are asking God to keep us from being tempted. This part of the Lord's Prayer means something like this: "Do not lead us into temptation, Lord; on the contrary, keep us as far away from it as possible."

Sometimes in his mercy God answers this prayer by keeping us from being tempted at all. However, sometimes God *does* allow us to be tempted. Therefore, "Lead us not into temptation" must be something more than a request not to be tempted. What we are really asking is for God to save us when we are tempted. God may not keep us from being tempted at all, but he can keep us from falling under temptation's power. Thus we are to pray that God will spare us from the satanic attacks that we are unable to withstand. "Do not let us be overcome by temptation, Lord!" "Protect us from being drawn into sin!" "Keep us from succumbing to Satan!"

By praying this way, we acknowledge both our own weakness and the strength of our enemy. We admit how likely we are to fall into sin. Yet we beg God not to allow us to do so, to keep us from being tempted beyond what we can bear. We pray that God will not abandon us, but will send us the help of the Holy Spirit. We trust him to be faithful to this promise: "He will not let you be tempted beyond what you can bear. But when you are tempted, he will also provide a way out so that you can stand up under it" (1 Cor. 10:13).

TEMPTED IN EVERY WAY

We may be sure that God will answer our prayer not to be led into temptation. God answers all our prayers, of course, one way or another. But we have special reason to believe that he will answer our prayer not to be led into temptation. Jesus knows all about our temptations and can explain them to his Father: "For we do not have a high priest who is unable to sympathize with our weaknesses, but we have one who has been tempted in every way, just as we are—yet without sin" (Heb. 4:15).

Jesus knows about our temptations because he has experienced every last one of them. He experienced them without ever giving in to them, which is why he was able to offer a perfect sacrifice for our sins. Now, whatever the temptation, Jesus can say, "Been there; resisted that." Having experienced all our temptations, he is also able to sympathize with our weakness. Since he understands our temptations, he also is able to understand what we mean when we pray, "Lead us not into temptation." He not only understands that prayer, but he also repeats it, for even now he stands at the right hand of the Father, interceding for us to be preserved from temptation.

We may be sure, therefore, that when we pray, "Lead us not into temptation," God will answer our prayers. For we are using a petition taught and tested by our Lord Jesus, a petition that he comprehends and communicates to the Father. "Let us then approach the throne of grace with confidence, so that we may receive mercy and find grace to help us in our time of need" (Heb. 5:16).

Charles Spurgeon once told a story about a man who received mercy and found grace in his time of need. The story came from the days of the English Reformation.

History records the fate of two men who were condemned to die in the burning days of Queen Mary. One of them boasted very loudly to his companions of his confidence that he would stand firm at the stake. He did not mind the suffering; he was so grounded in the gospel that he knew he would never deny it. . . .

His companion in prison in the same chamber was a poor trembling soul who could not and would not deny his Master; but he told his companion that he was very much afraid of the fire. He said . . . he was in great dread that when he began to burn, the pain might cause him to deny the truth. He besought his friend to pray for him, and he spent his time in very much weeping over his weakness and in crying to God for strength. . . .

When they both came to the stake, he who had been so bold recanted at the sight of the fire and went back ignominiously to an apostate's life, while the poor trembling man whose prayer had been *"Lead me not into temptation"* stood firm as a rock, praising and magnifying God as he was burnt to a cinder.[1]

It was the man who knew his own frailty who glorified God. He knew that he was weak, that his enemy was strong, and that only God could save him. So he prayed, "Lead me not into temptation," and God answered his prayer.

10

DELIVER US FROM THE EVIL ONE

We live in an evil world, so the last thing we ask in the Lord's Prayer is for God to deliver us: "Lead us not into temptation, but deliver us from the evil one." The word *but* ties both requests together. Not only do we ask God to keep us from evil, but we also ask him to rescue us when evil comes.

WHO IS THE EVIL ONE?

Notice that Jesus did not say simply, "Deliver us from evil." That is how the King James Version expresses it, and thus it is the way many people recite the Lord's Prayer. However, most modern translations say, "Deliver us from the evil *one*," which is more accurate. Most often when the New Testament speaks of "the evil one," it is speaking of Satan. He is "the evil one" who snatches away the good seed of God's Word (Matt. 13:19), who sows weeds next to God's wheat (13:38-39), and who has to be resisted with the shield of faith (Eph. 6:16). Behind everything and everyone evil there stands the devil himself—the Evil One.

Do you believe in the personal existence of Satan? Jesus certainly did. After all, he faced Satan's direct diabolical attacks in the wilderness (Matt. 4:1-11). Then, having withstood the full force of those temptations, Jesus taught his disciples to pray against the Evil One whenever they prayed. Unless we believe in the reality of the devil, as Jesus did, we will not see the need to pray against him. Evil is not a mysterious cosmic force, a kind of supernatural "dark side." No, behind every evil thing is a malignant, malevolent being who hates God and all his creatures.

It is from this Evil One that we need to be delivered. To "deliver" is to lead someone out of danger, the way God led the children of Israel out of slavery in Egypt. When we pray, therefore, we are asking God to rescue us from all the attacks of Satan. We are praying that when we face evil—as we must—God will lead us out of it.

THE HISTORY OF THE EVIL ONE

If we are not to be overcome by the Evil One, we must be aware of two dangers. One is to minimize Satan's importance by failing to recognize that he has real spiritual power. The other danger is to exaggerate his importance, becoming spell-bound by his sinister schemes.

The devil is a deceiver. He wants to make us believe that he isn't real. As the French poet Charles Baudelaire once wrote, "The devil's cleverest ruse is to make men believe that he does not exist."[1] Satan wants to give us the false impression that he is a silly old man in a red suit with little horns and a forked tail—or to convince us that his devilish powers are so overwhelming that we are helpless to resist.

The best way to counter these diabolical lies is with biblical truth. What does the Bible teach about the Evil One? The biography of Satan begins in heaven, where he was created to serve as one of God's most beautiful angels. But after a time Satan rebelled against the King of Heaven. He refused to give God the glory because he wanted it all for himself. Therefore, God cast him down from heaven (Rev. 12:13; Luke 10:18). The Evil One then vowed to hate God and to loathe him forever. From that time forward, he has tried to destroy God's work, particularly his special plan to save his people.

Satan began by tempting Adam and Eve in the Garden of Eden. He lied to the woman, telling her that eating the forbidden fruit would make her godlike (Gen. 3:5). By persuading her to sin, he also brought death to the human race. But almost as soon as humanity fell into sin, God promised to send a Savior who would bring Satan to absolute ruin (Gen. 3:15). As Satan slithered away from the garden, he determined to do everything in his power to stop that Savior from ever coming. All through the Old Testament, he tried to kill off the seed of the woman. Cain murdered Abel. Ishmael hated Isaac. Esau contended against Jacob. Saul tried to assassinate David. It was all part of the Evil One's desperate attempt to abort God's plan of salvation.

Satan failed. In the fullness of time, the promised Savior was born of a virgin. At that point, having failed to prevent his coming, the only thing Satan could do was try to keep him from accomplishing his saving purpose. So the Evil One went out into the wilderness, and there he tempted Jesus to use his deity to his own advantage, to win the kingdom without enduring the cross.

Jesus resisted every temptation. Yet the battle was not yet finished, because Scripture says that "when the devil had finished all this tempting, he left him until an opportune time" (Luke 4:13). Afterwards we see him skulking in the shadows of the Gospels, looking for a chance to get rid of Jesus once and for all. Satan took his chance when Judas Iscariot went to the Jewish authorities and offered to betray Jesus (Luke 22:3-4). The Evil One worked his plan to perfection. In rapid succession Jesus was betrayed, arrested, beaten, crucified, and buried.

Except the plan didn't work after all. Jesus rose from the dead. The most that Satan could do was to bruise the Savior's heel. And then by his resurrection, Jesus gained a crushing victory over sin, death, and the devil.

THE STRATEGIES OF THE EVIL ONE

The Evil One has not given up the fight, however. Having failed to defeat Christ, he now tries to defeat the Christian. And since he is our most hateful enemy, we should beware of his tactics. The Bible teaches that when Satan "saw that he had been hurled to the earth," he "went off to make war against . . . those who obey God's commandments and hold to the testimony of Jesus" (Rev. 12:13, 17).

As Satan continues to wage this invisible war, he has many weapons at his disposal. First, there is *domination*. Satan is the Dominator. The Bible teaches that sinners who have not yet come to faith in Christ are "under the power of the devil" (Acts 10:38). By serving themselves, rather than serving God, they are actually serving Satan. Whether they realize it or not, the devil "has taken them captive to do his will" (2 Tim. 2:26). Apart from Christ, therefore, the human race is dominated by the Evil One. Wherever there is greed, deception, hatred, or violence, the devil has established his deadly dominion.

Another weapon of the Evil One is *temptation*. Satan is the Tempter. Of all the weapons at his disposal, temptation is perhaps the oldest and most effective. It is the weapon Satan used against Eve in the Garden of Eden. It is the weapon he uses so often today, enticing people to look at pornographic images on the computer screen, to covet merchandise in the catalog, or to envy someone else's success.

Once we have fallen to temptation, the Evil One resorts

to *accusation*. Satan is the Accuser, the one who charges God's children with being unfaithful to their Father. Thus the Bible calls him "the accuser of our brothers, who accuses them before our God day and night" (Rev. 12:10b).

Then there is *confrontation*, meaning all the ways the Evil One opposes the Christian church. Satan stages a continual confrontation with the work of the Gospel. He is the Adversary, for that is what his name literally means. Satan confronts the church by teaching error and encouraging false worship. According to the Bible, it is the work of Satan that is "displayed in all kinds of counterfeit miracles, signs and wonders, and in every sort of evil that deceives those who are perishing" (2 Thess. 2:9b-10a). The Adversary uses these tricks to hinder the work of missions and evangelism.

Satan is very dangerous. He is the Dominator, the Tempter, the Accuser, and the Adversary. And these are only some of what John Calvin called "the violent assaults of Satan."[2] From the very beginning of the world, the Evil One has done everything in his power to destroy God's plan for his people. Sooner or later everyone is bedeviled by one or more of his weapons. Hence our need for the Lord's Prayer, in which we beg God to deliver us from evil.

DELIVERANCE!

There are times when evil cannot be escaped, when the only hope is deliverance. A good example comes from British history:

In the old English wars between the king and Parliament, the town of Taunton . . . sustained a long siege. Food rose to twenty times its market value. Half the houses were blown down by a storm of fire, and many of the people perished from hunger. Through all of this, the townsfolk had been accustomed to meet in St. Mary's Church to pray, and we may be sure that the burden of their daily prayers to the Father was, "Deliver us!" One day as they were assembled for this purpose, hoping to hear that the enemy had at last retreated, a trusty messenger came to the church door and spoke but one word, "Deliverance!" In a moment the magic word flew through the vast assembly, and all shouted with one voice, "Deliverance!"[3]

Deliverance! It is what God has guaranteed in his Gospel. We cannot withstand Satan in our own strength, but God has promised to lead us out of danger and save us from all the powers of evil. The Gospel is the word of deliverance. It is the good news God first announced in the Garden of Eden—that Satan's head would be crushed by the woman's seed (Gen. 3:15).

How did Jesus deliver us? He defeated the devil by dying on the cross and rising again from the dead. The plan was that "by his death he might destroy him who holds the power of death—that is, the devil" (Heb. 2:14b). When Jesus died on the cross, he paid the full penalty for our sins. When he rose from the dead, he gained victory over the grave. Therefore, by his crucifixion and resurrection, Jesus has saved us from sin and death. He has undone the work of the devil, who can no longer hold God's children under the power of sin and death.

As we have seen, the Evil One still has many weapons in his arsenal—domination, temptation, accusation, confrontation. But our crucified and risen Savior has a countermeasure for every demonic attack. The Evil One tries to dominate, but Jesus liberates, saving us from the devil's dominion: "For he has rescued us from the dominion of darkness and brought us into the kingdom of the Son he loves" (Col. 1:13). The Evil One tries to tempt us, but Jesus gives us the power to resist temptation. He showed us how to do it when he defeated the devil in the wilderness. Now he tells us to do the same thing: "Resist the devil, and he will flee from you" (James 4:7).

The Evil One tries to accuse us, but Jesus defends us with his own perfect record. When Satan charges that we are sinners, Jesus stands before his Father's throne and says, "They may be sinners, but I died for their sins." Then he holds out his hands to show how he was pierced for our transgressions. The Evil One also tries to confront the whole church, but Jesus is our rock and our fortress. One of the last things he prayed before his crucifixion was "Protect them from the evil one" (John 17:15). Now, as the church preaches and lives the Gospel, God answers that prayer. Even as Christians face hardship, opposition, persecution, and martyrdom, God is building his church so that the gates of hell will not prevail against it (Matt. 16:18).

Soon our warfare will be over, and Satan will no longer trouble us. Our commander, Jesus Christ, will call us away from the battlefield to receive the victor's crown. Then we will share in his absolute, eternal conquest of the Evil One, for as the Scripture has promised, "the God of peace will soon crush Satan under your feet" (Rom. 16:20a).

What more can we ask than the total defeat of evil and the Evil One? Cyprian said that "when we say, 'Deliver us from evil,' there remains nothing further which ought to be asked. When we have once asked for God's protection against evil, and have obtained it, then against everything which the devil and the world work against us we stand secure and safe."[4] Safe and secure we will remain, invincible in Christ for all eternity.

11

THE POWER AND
THE GLORY

The Lord's Prayer ends, not with another petition, but with a doxology: "For thine is the kingdom, and the power, and the glory, forever. Amen" (Matt. 6:13b KJV).

A BIBLICAL DOXOLOGY

Christians have prayed these words for nearly two thousand years, and yet there is some question as to whether they were part of the original Lord's Prayer or not. In the New International Version the prayer closes with the words "deliver us from the evil one" (Matt. 6:13). There is only a note in the margin to explain that some late manuscripts also include the words "for yours is the kingdom and the power and the glory forever. Amen."

The true situation is complicated, but it seems best to conclude that the traditional doxology was not part of the original text of Matthew but was in use from the early days of the church. It is not hard to guess how it might have come to be added. Jewish prayers of that time nearly always ended with words of praise. The most common Jewish doxology went: "Blessed be the name of the glory of his kingdom for ever and ever."[1] It would have been unthinkable for a Jew to offer a prayer in those days without some kind of doxology, especially a prayer that ended the way the Lord's Prayer ended, with the words "deliver us from the evil one." Rather than letting the Evil One have the last word, it must have seemed only natural to close with praise to God.

All of this still leaves us with a practical question, however: What should we do when we pray? Should we use the traditional doxology or not?

We may use the traditional doxology because it is biblical. What could be more biblical than ascribing the kingdom, the power, and the glory to God? This is the prayer that King David offered when God's people presented their offerings for building the temple:

> "Yours, O LORD, is the greatness and the power
> and the glory and the majesty and the splendor,
>   for everything in heaven and earth is yours.
> Yours, O LORD, is the kingdom;
>   you are exalted as head over all."

(1 CHRON. 29:11)

Therefore, whether it was given by Jesus or not, the traditional ending of the Lord's Prayer is part of the biblical pattern for prayer.

YOURS, O LORD, IS THE KINGDOM

First we praise God for his kingdom, declaring that he is ruler over all. David said, "Yours, O LORD, is the kingdom" (1 Chron. 29:11b).

We have prayed about the kingdom before. Near the beginning of the Lord's Prayer, we learned about the plan, the purpose, and the progress of God's kingdom. God's plan is to establish his kingdom through the preaching of the cross. His purpose is to rule in the hearts of his people. The progress of this spiritual kingdom will be steady but slow. In one sense, the kingdom has already come with the death and resurrection of Jesus Christ. Now it continues to grow as his cross and his empty tomb are preached in all the world.

There is another sense, however, in which we are still looking for the kingdom, waiting for the King to come again. We live in the kingdom of grace, where Christ rules by faith, but we wait for the kingdom of glory, when Christ will reign supreme over all.

The doxology at the end of the Lord's Prayer mentions the kingdom again; only this time it says something slightly different. Back in the second petition we prayed for the kingdom to come. In the doxology we acknowledge that God is *already* the King. Jesus is the King; where he is, the kingdom is. Therefore, what the Lord's Prayer says is simply a fact:

"Thine *is* the kingdom." Even now Jesus sits at the right hand of God in the place of absolute authority over earth and heaven.

At the same time that we pray for God's kingdom to come in all its fullness, we praise God that he is already the King. Here at the end of the Lord's Prayer, we acknowledge God as sovereign over everything in heaven and earth. We claim Jesus as our own King, the ruler of our thoughts, actions, and emotions. And as we pray, his kingdom comes. For when we pray, "Thine is the kingdom," God establishes his rule over our prayers, and thus over our hearts.

YOURS, O LORD, IS THE POWER

Not every king has as much power as he would like. The kingdoms of this world have always been limited monarchies. But the King who reigns above is the Lord God Almighty. His power is absolute, "for the Lord God omnipotent reigneth" (Rev. 19:6 KJV). Hence we pray, as David prayed, "Yours, O LORD, is the power."

There is one kind of divine power that seems especially important here at the close of the Lord's Prayer, and that is God's power to answer prayer. We depend on that power for each and every one of our petitions. We pray, "Our Father which art in heaven, hallowed be thy name." By doing so, we trust that God has the power to hallow his name, to show by the worship of angels and humans that he is the holy, holy, holy God. We pray, "Thy kingdom come," trusting that through the preaching of the Gospel and the conversion of sinners, God's Spirit will spread God's rule through all the earth. "Thy will be done," we pray, "on earth as it is in heaven." Then we wait for God to work out his purpose, believing that he has the power to do whatever he wills.

Having prayed for God's name, God's rule, and God's will, we begin to pray for our own needs. We know that God has the power to provide food, clothing, and shelter, and so we pray, "Give us this day our daily bread." Then we trust him to provide everything we need. We also ask God to "forgive us our debts," trusting that he has the power to take away our sin through the cross of Christ. Last of all, we pray for God to deliver us from the temptations of the Evil One, and thus to show his absolute power over the devil.

We confess the omnipotence of God every time we say, "For thine is . . . the power." The word *for* establishes the connection between the rest of the Lord's Prayer and the doxology. It grounds our petitions in our praise. First comes our long list of requests. On what basis do we expect God to grant them? "*For* thine is the power." This is a statement of our faith. It acknowledges our utter dependence on divine grace for everything we need, and it expresses our absolute confidence in God's ability to hear us and help us.

Yours, O Lord, Is the Glory

Once we have been brought into God's kingdom and have seen his power, the only appropriate way for us to respond is by giving him the glory. The word *glory* comes from the Hebrew term for "heavy," and thus "signifies gravity, heaviness, greatness, and abundance."[2] When we speak of the glory of God, then, we refer first to the internal weight of his character. Glory is the "excellency, dignity, and worthiness" of God. It is not so much a divine attribute in itself as it is the cumulative weight of all God's attributes. Glory is the gravity of God's being.

God does not keep the weight of his glory to himself, however, which brings us to a second meaning of the word. "Glory," wrote Jonathan Edwards, "is also the outshining of the internal greatness or excellence. The word *glory* is used in Scripture often to express the *exhibition, emanation,* or *communication* of the internal glory. Hence it often signifies an effulgence, or shining brightness, by an emanation of beams of light."[3]

The most spectacular display of God's glory is through his Son Jesus Christ. God the Son became a man so that we could see the glory of God. He revealed God's glory in many ways, but especially by suffering and dying on the cross for our sins. In his death and resurrection, Jesus made the most amazing display of God's love and justice, demonstrating the glory of God in the salvation of sinners.

The reason Jesus saved us was so that we would glorify God. This is the third way the Bible speaks of glory. First, glory is the inward majesty of God; second, it is the brightness God sometimes shines out into the world; third, it is the worship we offer to God. When we see God's glory, the proper way for us to respond is to give him the glory—to offer him all the honor and praise he deserves. To God alone be the glory!

FOREVER AND EVER, AMEN!

"Yours is the kingdom and the power and the glory forever"— this traditional doxology is a fitting way to end the Lord's Prayer. It lifts our minds and hearts to the glorious throne where God rules the universe by his grace and power. Thus our prayer ends where it began, by giving worship to God alone.

The last word of the Lord's Prayer is "amen," the Hebrew word that means "I agree," or "so be it." Saying "Amen!" is a way of testifying that something is true. As Martin Luther once said, "It is a word uttered by the firm faith of the heart," a word used to affirm "something that is most certainly true."[4]

The "Amen" at the end of the Lord's Prayer is not an afterthought. In a way, it is the most important word in the whole prayer, because it makes the prayer our own. We are saying, "Yes, Lord, this is our prayer, and we mean it with all our hearts."

William Willimon and Stanley Hauerwas of Duke University recount a true story that illustrates the power of an "Amen":

In a prison camp in World War II, on a cold, dark evening after a series of beatings, after the hundreds of prisoners of war had been marched before the camp commander and harangued for an hour, when the prisoners were returned to their dark barracks and told to be quiet for the rest of the night, someone, somewhere in one of the barracks began saying the Lord's Prayer. Some of his fellow prisoners lying next to him began to pray with him. Their prayer was overheard by prisoners in the next building who joined them. One by one, each set of barracks joined in the prayer until, as the prayer was ending with, "Thine is the kingdom, the power, and the glory," hundreds of prisoners had joined their voices in a strong, growing, defiant prayer, reaching a thunderous "Amen!"[5]

That war story is a picture of what we do when we pray the way Jesus taught us to pray. We offer our prayers from the barracks, for we are still at war with our old enemy, the devil. Soon our warfare will be over, and Christ will reign victoriously. But in the meantime it is cold and dark, and we must take courage by praying together. Right at the end of our prayers, we give God the glory for the power of his eternal kingdom, and then we say, "Amen!"

Charles Wesley once took the traditional conclusion to the Lord's Prayer and turned it into verse. His words provide a fitting doxology to this book on prayer:

> *Yea, Amen! Let all adore thee,*
> *High on thine eternal throne;*
> *Saviour, take the power and glory:*
> *Claim the Kingdom for thine own:*
> *O come quickly!*
> *Alleluia! Come, Lord, come!*

NOTES

FOREWORD

1   Quoted from Lisa Beamer's Foreword in *A Reason for Hope* (Wheaton, IL.: Crossway Books, 2001), pp. 10, 11.

CHAPTER 1: HOW TO PRAY

1   Hugh Latimer, quoted in Spiros Zodhiates, *The Lord's Prayer*, rev. ed. (Chattanooga, Tenn.: AMG, 1991), 28.

2   Zodhiates, vii.

CHAPTER 2: OUR FATHER IN HEAVEN

1   R. Kent Hughes, *Abba Father: The Lord's Pattern for Prayer* (Wheaton, Ill.: Crossway, 1986), 17-18.

2   David Blankenhorn, *Fatherless America: Confronting Our Most Urgent Social Problem* (New York: HarperCollins, 1995).

3   James Barr, "Abba Isn't 'Daddy,'" *Journal of Theological Studies*, 39 (1988): 28-47.

4   Robert H. Gundry, *Matthew: A Commentary on His Handbook for a Mixed Church Under Persecution*, 2nd ed. (Grand Rapids, Mich.: Eerdmans, 1994), 105.

CHAPTER 3: HOLY IS YOUR NAME

1   Thomas Watson, *The Lord's Prayer* (1692; repr. Edinburgh: Banner of Truth, 1960), 38.

CHAPTER 5: YOUR WILL BE DONE

1   Robert Coles, *The Spiritual Life of Children* (Boston: Houghton Mifflin, 1990), xiv.

2   Betty Scott Stam, quoted in Elisabeth Elliott, "Glorifying God in Mission," *Evangelicals Now* (November 1998), 9.

3   John Wesley, quoted in *The Methodist Service Book* (London: Methodist Publishing House, 1975), D10.

CHAPTER 6: GIVE US TODAY OUR DAILY BREAD

1   Don Brothy, "Why I Don't Pray Anymore," *National Catholic Reporter* (March 1, 1974), 9.

2   Brian J. Dodd, *Praying Jesus' Way: A Guide for Beginners and Veterans* (Downers Grove, Ill.: InterVarsity, 1997), 91, 128.

3   Gregory of Nyssa, quoted in Herman Witsius, *Dissertations on the Lord's Prayer* (Edinburgh, 1839; repr. Escondido, Calif.: Den Dulk Christian Foundation, 1994), 295-96.

4   Hudson Taylor, quoted in Marshall Broomhall, *The Man Who Believed God: The Story of Hudson Taylor* (Chicago: Moody, 1929), 150.

CHAPTER 7: FORGIVE US OUR DEBTS

1   Spiros Zodhiates, *The Lord's Prayer*, rev. ed. (Chattanooga, Tenn.: AMG, 1991), 229.

CHAPTER 8: AS WE FORGIVE OUR DEBTORS

1   R. Kent Hughes, *Abba Father: The Lord's Pattern for Prayer* (Wheaton, Ill.: Crossway, 1986), 79.

2   George Herbert, quoted in William H. Willimon and Stanley
     Hauerwas, *Lord, Teach Us: The Lord's Prayer and the Christian Life*
     (Nashville, Tenn.: Abingdon, 1996), 83.

3   Richard Wurmbrand, "Give a Gem at Christmas," *The Voice of the
     Martyrs* (December 1998), 14.

CHAPTER 9: LEAD US NOT INTO TEMPTATION

1   Charles Haddon Spurgeon, *The Metropolitan Tabernacle Pulpit*, 63
     vols. (Pasadena, Texas: Pilgrim, 1969), 24:143, as retold by R. Kent
     Hughes in *Abba Father: The Lord's Pattern for Prayer* (Wheaton, Ill.:
     Crossway, 1986), 92-93.

CHAPTER 10: DELIVER US FROM THE EVIL ONE

1   Charles Baudelaire, quoted in Donald Grey Barnhouse, *The Invisible
     War* (Grand Rapids, Mich.: Zondervan, 1965), 156.

2   John Calvin, *Institutes of the Christian Religion*, trans. Ford Lewis
     Battles, 2 vols., Library of Christian Classics, 20-21 (Philadelphia,
     Pa.: Westminster, 1960), III.xx.46.

3   Spiros Zodhiates, *The Lord's Prayer*, rev. ed. (Chattanooga, Tenn.:
     AMG, 1991), 295.

4   Cyprian, "Treatise on the Lord's Prayer," in *Hippolytus, Cyprian,
     Caius, Novatian, Appendix*, ed. Alexander Roberts and James
     Donaldson, Ante-Nicene Fathers, 10 vols. (Christian Literature,
     1886; repr. Peabody, Mass.: Hendrickson, 1994), 5:455.

CHAPTER 11: THE POWER AND THE GLORY

1   Herman Witsius, *Dissertations on the Lord's Prayer* (Edinburgh,
     1839; repr. Escondido, Calif.: Den Dulk Christian Foundation,
     1994), 376.

2   Jonathan Edwards, "The End for Which God Created the World,"
     reprinted in John Piper, *God's Passion for His Glory* (Wheaton, Ill.:
     Crossway, 1998), 230.

3   Edwards, quoted in Piper, ibid., 233.

4   Martin Luther, "An Exposition of the Lord's Prayer for Simple
     Laymen, 1519," trans. Martin H. Bertram, in *Devotional Writings I*,
     ed. Martin O. Dietrich, *Luther's Works*, 55 vols. (Philadelphia, Pa.:
     Fortress, 1969), 42:76-77.

5   William H. Willimon and Stanley Hauerwas, *Lord, Teach Us: The
     Lord's Prayer and the Christian Life* (Nashville, Tenn.: Abingdon,
     1996), 108-109.